Praise for
John Hall and *Top of Mind*

"John's got his finger on something here—something important. Anyone interested in communicating effectively through content would do well to embrace the audience-centric approach outlined in *Top of Mind*."

—Eric Hellweg, managing director at
Harvard Business Review

"*Top of Mind* is a critical and powerful tool to catapult yourself into relevance in a noisy, competitive world. Get it now, and leverage your content like never before."

—Jeff Hoffman, cofounder of
Priceline and ColorJar

"With *Top of Mind*, John breaks down the last barriers between executives and content marketing. We accept that business is about relationships, and it's time we embrace the fact that the right content at the right time can make those relationships (and your company) stronger."

—Evan Greene, CMO of The Recording Academy
(The GRAMMYs)

"John Hall says that success ultimately comes down to creating meaningful relationships—in business and in life. I couldn't agree more. Buy this book to get his prescription for exactly how to do it."

—Ann Handley, chief content officer of
MarketingProfs and author of *Everybody Writes*

"This is the playbook for how to make yourself memorable online. *Top of Mind* is useful, practical, and vital. Highly recommended!"
—Jay Baer, president of Convince & Convert
and author of *Hug Your Haters*

"An absolute must-read for any professional or company seeking to build influence and lead their industry."
—Forbes.com

"Potential customers can't do business with you if they don't even know who you are. John Hall's essential new book shows you how to powerfully connect with your audience, even in today's crowded marketplace, so the right business opportunities come to you."
—Dorie Clark, author of
Reinventing You and *Stand Out*

"I am a longtime admirer of John's knack for connecting people in meaningful—sometimes life- and career-changing—ways. The idea of 'shifting from self to the people who matter' is something he practices personally and professionally, so all ideas in the book are authentic and tested. *Top of Mind* contains John's simple, yet powerful, secret to success. Readers will be grateful he shared it!"
—Gina McDuffie, CMO of VER

"Here it is, a business guide to engineering serendipity! *Top of Mind* is a relationship guide for the digital age. Whether you're building a business or accelerating your career, John Hall's clever concept and smart insight will transform the way you communicate. Move over, Mr. Carnegie; John Hall teaches anyone how to win friends and influence people—at massive scale."
—Andrew M. Davis, founder of Monumental
Shift and author of *Brandscaping*

"*Top of Mind* is a must-read for any business professional who wants to understand how to break through the noisy and competitive landscape of today's digital, social, and mobile world. As an innovative and successful entrepreneur, John Hall shows us how anyone in any type of business can use their existing knowledge and expertise to become top of mind, reach potential customers, and grow their business."

—MICHAEL BRENNER, CEO of Marketing Insider
Group and author of *The Content Formula*

TOP

OF

MIND

TOP

OF

MIND

USE CONTENT TO UNLEASH YOUR INFLUENCE
AND ENGAGE THOSE WHO MATTER TO YOU

JOHN HALL

NEW YORK   CHICAGO   SAN FRANCISCO   ATHENS
LONDON   MADRID   MEXICO CITY   MILAN
NEW DELHI   SINGAPORE   SYDNEY   TORONTO

1 2 3 4 5 6 7 8 9   LCR   22 21 20 19 18 17

ISBN 978-1-260-01192-0
MHID   1-260-01192-5

e-ISBN 978-1-260-01193-7
e-MHID   1-260-01193-3

Design by Mauna Eichner and Lee Fukui

Library of Congress Cataloging-in-Publication Data

Names: Hall, John Michael, author.
Title: Top of mind : use content to unleash your influence and engage those
  who matter to you / John Hall.
Description: 1 Edition. | New York : McGraw-Hill Education, 2017.
Identifiers: LCCN 2016057879 (print) | LCCN 2017011153 (ebook) | ISBN
  9781260011920 (hardback) | ISBN 1260011925 | ISBN 9781260011937 () | ISBN
  1260011933
Subjects: LCSH: Consumers—Research. | Consumers—Information services. |
  BISAC: BUSINESS & ECONOMICS / Marketing / General.
Classification: LCC HF5415.32 .H355 2017 (print) | LCC HF5415.32 (ebook) |
  DDC 658.8/343—dc23
LC record available at https://lccn.loc.gov/2016057879

McGraw-Hill Education books are available at special quantity discounts to use as premiums and sales promotions or for use in corporate training programs. To contact a representative, please visit the Contact Us pages at www.mhprofessional .com.

To all the writers, editors, and other creatives

behind many of the best pieces of content

who don't get the credit they deserve

CONTENTS

FOREWORD

ONE OF MY business heroes is Professor Don Schultz at Northwestern University. I was introduced to Don's work when I first began my career in the publishing industry nearly 20 years ago. When most marketers and thought leaders were talking about the 4Ps as critical to marketing, Don was talking about one thing: communication as differentiation.

Professor Schultz—known today as the father of integrated marketing—said that our competitors can copy everything we do as an organization: they can copy our products, our services, our processes. The only thing they can't copy is how we communicate.

Just think about that for a second. In my journeys, the majority of enterprises I meet with are focusing on everything BUT their communications. In this age of massive technological change in which artificial intelligence and instant communication are becoming the norm, those few companies that communicate valuable, consistent information in an authentic manner win.

It really is that simple.

Sure, I love to read books about automation and new ways to segment and target an audience, but if it doesn't lead to a behavior change in that audience, it's all for nothing. This is the exact reason why you need to take this book and hold it tight against you (I'm not kidding).

So before you crack this baby open and change your stars, consider these questions:

▲ Am I delivering real value to my customers every day outside the products and services that I offer?

▲ Do I understand the real needs and pain points of my customers and prospects?

▲ If my customers are having a significant problem, would they think of and contact me first?

▲ Do my customers like and trust me?

If you answered "yes" to these questions, this book will be a refresher. But in my experience, less than 1 percent of all companies can answer these questions in the affirmative. Take all the other marketing BS away and these are the questions that really matter. Make getting to "yes" on these questions a priority.

How are you delivering real, tangible value to your customers in how you communicate? That's what matters . . . now and 50 years from now.

Just remember, people don't care about your products and services; they care about their needs. If you can't have a conversation with them about their pain points, you'll never get them to consistently buy from you.

Start that conversation today by diving into this book. I promise you it will *change your stars* forever.

JOE PULIZZI
Founder of the Content Marketing Institute
Bestselling author of *Epic Content Marketing*
and *Content Inc.*

ACKNOWLEDGMENTS

BEN LOSMAN, YOU are truly one of the most talented writers with a creative mind who expertly shapes words to tell a more engaging story.

To the amazing team of women who helped edit and craft this book to be the best version it could be:

Nickie Bartels

Natalie Slyman

Taylor Oster

Kelsey Meyer

Casey Ebro

To my family and friends, I believe you are at your best when you surround yourself with amazing people in your personal and professional life. I can honestly say that I am truly blessed.

INTRODUCTION

You're sitting at your desk when, for some reason, you find yourself thinking about your best friend from fifth grade. You realize that it's been years since you last spoke. Just as you begin tripping down memory lane, feeling guilty about losing touch with someone who was, at one time, so important to you, an e-mail arrives in your inbox. The first lines read:

> Hey, I know this might sound weird, but I was just sitting here at work when you popped into my mind out of nowhere. I can't believe it's been so long! How've you been since fifth grade?

I don't care how jaded or cynical you are—when you're randomly thinking about someone and that person's name suddenly materializes in your inbox, you're going to experience a moment of childlike wonder. For a full second or two after that e-mail appears, you'll contemplate whether you can control space-time with your mind. (Once you realize how ridiculous that sounds, you'll focus on more plausible questions, such as whether you're being *Inception*ed.)

As humans, we're fascinated by coincidences like this one because they are filled with possibility. Carl Jung believed that such moments of synchronicity reveal hidden truths about the universe. Others interpret coincidence through the lens of religion, spirituality, or science. Even the most skeptical interpretation—that an unexpected yet meaningful occurrence merely represents a statistical improbability—is still based on the desire to find an explanation.

When the person you're thinking of suddenly appears, is it a message from the universe? Or is it simply random chance?

I have no idea. What I do know is that there is tremendous potential in the statement "Oh, my God! I was just thinking of you!"

In fact, most of my success in business—and in life—hinges on that phrase and the magical feeling that comes with it. Because if you can get the right people to think of you at the right times, you can accomplish great things.

We process an incredible amount of information every second. So many of our judgments and decisions, from the strategic to the mundane, come down to the information we can call to our conscious minds in an instant. By ensuring that you are top of mind among the people in your networks making those important decisions, you are positioning yourself for success.

For example, let's say you run a software development company. If potential clients are already thinking about you at the moment they begin looking for a vendor that can deliver software that meets their needs, you are at a distinct competitive advantage. Unlike competing companies that are trying to cut through the noise and the clutter and the trust barriers that slow down sales and partnerships, you are already on top of the potential clients' mind—and that's powerful.

It isn't enough to come to their mind as just another vendor, though. You want them to view you as a partner and a resource that they value and trust. And there, at the intersection of timing and trust, is your opportunity to influence decision makers.

Apply this scenario to current and potential partners, investors, media contacts, and employees. Imagine the impact that widespread top-of-mind status can have on your growth.

In this book, you'll learn how to engage and position yourself on top of the minds of the people who matter most—so that whenever opportunity arises, they'll already be thinking of you.

Not long ago, I sent an e-mail to the CEO of a midmarket firm wishing him a happy Thanksgiving. This wasn't someone I knew particularly well—he and I had met only once, and we had never had a real conversation—but within half an hour, I'd received a reply.

"John, total coincidence. I was literally just thinking about you. My team and I are about to discuss the keynote for our conference next year, and I think you should be the speaker. Interested?"

Strange, right? Was this the universe itself endorsing me as a candidate for this conference's keynote speaker? Maybe. I mean, after all, the only thing I did to elicit an invitation was wish him a happy Thanksgiving.

But my "Happy Thanksgiving" e-mail didn't really come from out of the blue. I had sent this man personal greetings on every public holiday for more than a year; this was simply the first time he had responded.

Later, I discovered that he was a regular reader of my *Forbes* column on leadership, content marketing, and online PR—and he was especially fond of the article in which I named his company's conference as one of the most important of the year. And, finally, he had actually seen me speak a few months earlier at a different conference.

Over time, my diverse branding efforts had helped me make my way to the top of his mind. That's not to imply that every time he closed his eyes, he saw my face. (And, truthfully, I probably wouldn't accept an invitation from such an individual.)

In all seriousness, he probably wasn't even aware that he had been thinking about me. I imagine it went something more like this: Picture his brain as an office. Because he had regularly been seeing my name attached to things he liked (my columns, the conference speech I gave, and genuine holiday greetings), I wasn't tucked away in a folder at the bottom of some dark subconscious filing cabinet; I was at the very top of a pile of memories that lay just beneath his conscious mind. When it came time to do the mental work of finding a keynote speaker for his conference, I was one of the easiest memories to retrieve.

See? Nothing as mysterious as the forces of the universe; nothing as manipulative as *Inception*. All I had to do was be myself and treat him in a way that I'd want to be treated, and everything fell into place.

Sure, this is a simple example, but it represents the essence of this book—as well as my entire business and personal philosophy. I've learned that when you make life better for other people and treat them with respect, they appreciate you. And because they appreciate you, they think about you. Cultivate appreciation, and it becomes opportunity.

In this book, you'll learn how to create opportunity for yourself personally and professionally by developing top-of-mind status among those who matter most to you.

Chapters 1 and 2 describe the major shifts in today's consumer landscape and why a top-of-mind strategy is essential for achieving competitive advantage for any audience. Chapters 3 through 5 explain how to build an authentic, transparent, and consistent personal brand that serves others just as well as it serves you—because if your brand isn't genuine, it's a liability. And in Chapters 6 through 10, you'll learn how to enrich the lives of your target audience, whoever it's made up of, through high-quality digital content that builds trust and creates meaningful human connections between your brand and the world.

Through years of experience practicing this philosophy, I've learned a lot about what it takes to become top of mind, and I've come to rely on content to help me scale my efforts.

You can practice any number of tactics with a top-of-mind mindset, such as your personal interactions or one-on-one communications with different members of your audience. But these habits aren't scalable. You have only so much time in a day or a week or a year, and you can be in only one place at a time. You cannot possibly interact personally with each individual member of your audience with whom you'd like to build trust. It's just not physically possible.

Building those relationships is still important, but if you can't rely on individual interactions to develop them, you have to practice another tactic—and that's where content comes into the picture.

So if at any point in this book you start to wonder why I reference digital content, it's because much of the success I've seen has come from creating written content and then distributing it to audiences online, interacting with followers and influencers on social media, and speaking at events.

These types of content have been a core part of my top-of-mind strategy because they give me the chance to build trust and relationships with an audience I would otherwise never have been able to reach at once. They've also helped me grow personally and professionally.

Because this top-of-mind practice has worked so well for me and others I've worked with, I want to share my stories, my lessons, and my tactics with you so that you, too, might better understand the unique role of content in placing you top of mind. Once you learn why and how a top-of-mind strategy works to create opportunity, you'll learn exactly how digital content can help you earn, maintain, and scale that opportunity—and you'll gain a tactical understanding of how to put it into practice.

Ultimately, everything in life comes down to establishing and maintaining meaningful human connections. Therefore, the techniques I'll be discussing will be just as relevant to growing your startup as they will be to raising your kids or pursuing your lifelong goals.

I've certainly found them helpful, and I hope you do, too.

1

HOW YOUR CONSUMERS ARE CHANGING

THE YEAR IS 1995. It's daybreak in Illinois, and Peoria's most promising young salesperson is already up and preparing for the day. What he lacks in experience he makes up for in enthusiasm. As he gels his hair, he rehearses his pitch in front of the mirror.

"Hello, ma'am. My name is John, and you may think you know popcorn, but you've never tasted popcorn until you've tried this. If you'd just invite me in, I'd be happy to share a free sample. . . ."

I remember my teenage door-to-door sales days as if they were yesterday. Unlike most of my popcorn-hawking peers, I really enjoyed this job. When I think about it, I can still feel the excitement that began with ringing a doorbell and ended with closing a sale. Never mind that the popcorn (or sausage and cheese, or cookies, or whatever the faceless distributor had its young mercenaries pushing that week) was grotesquely overpriced; that didn't matter. Put any kind of processed food in my hands, and I could sing its praises for hours. And if people happened to be listening, they'd probably end up buying it.

But the thought of doing door-to-door today makes me cringe.

"Ma'am, my name is John, and you may think you know popcorn, but..."

"Now hold on just a minute, John. I read an article about the risks of eating too much popcorn, and I don't know if I'm ready to buy this much just yet. Besides, the reviews are terrible! And people aren't too thrilled about you, either. See? *Cute but pushy. Free sample not worth it.* Sorry, kid. Keep walking."

I didn't realize it then, but as I was working on my teenage sales chops, the era of "Me Marketing" was coming to a close.

Throughout most of the twentieth century, the marketing, sales, and advertising spotlight was firmly planted on the product and the person selling it. Charisma was currency. The consumer wasn't an individual capable of independent thought; she or he was an object to be talked at and sold to.

Why did the disciples of Don Draper take such a condescending view of their customers? Because, for decades, it worked. An aggressive pitch was the shortest distance between a brand interaction and a sale.

And then the information revolution transformed life as we know it.

From a business perspective, the Internet reshaped the consumer landscape completely. Suddenly, consumers had immediate access to product data, customer reviews, and trusted opinions. Connectivity empowered people to make informed, deliberate purchasing decisions. Instead of being seduced by a charismatic sales pitch (or a cute but pushy young salesperson), consumers could decide whether a product would fit their individual needs, desires, and lifestyle before ever laying hands on it.

You might think that such a dramatic shift in power from the seller to the consumer would kill off Me Marketing—but you'd be wrong.

In fact, Internet-era Me Marketing is a thriving, multi-billion-dollar industry, one defended by its advocates as more effective than ever.

When was the last time you clicked on a banner ad? How many times this week have you pored through your spam folder, credit card in hand, just cruising for a good deal?

Rather than disappearing, Me Marketing has actually intensified its efforts to capture and control our attention spans. To be alive today is to face a constant barrage of aggressive, annoying ads and pitches. They elbow for position in your inbox, Twitter feed, and favorite news sites. They interrupt the podcasts you're listening to, and they bog down the apps you download. They punch you in the face every time you visit a website so you can't access the content you want until you click them away.

To survive, we've become experts at tuning out the noise. And we've turned to technology for help.

According to *Business Insider*, the number of monthly active users of ad blocking software approached 200 million in 2015.[1] That marks a 48 percent increase from the year before.[2]

These numbers have both advertisers and publishers panicked because digital ad revenue fuels the Internet. But one look at our melting icecaps will prove that utter dependence on an unsustainable fuel source leads to catastrophe.

My point is not that advertising is inherently obsolete; there are plenty of creative people doing compelling, effective work through traditional and new ad media. However, a traditional advertising *mindset*—one based on the Me Marketing philosophy—is not only obsolete; it's a liability. Because when you annoy your customer base, you alienate the people who matter most.

The same holds true in sales, as well as in personal branding. When was the last time an aggressive vendor irritated you to the point of not wanting to engage with his company? Or when the narcissism of a CEO's social media profile made you reconsider partnering with her?

Just because your customers are posting gigabytes worth of duck-faced selfies doesn't mean you should be doing the equivalent with your brand. To be successful, you need to shift your focus from yourself and your product or service outward onto the people who matter.

It's Not Me, It's You

The Internet, social media, and mobile technology—not to mention the scars we all carry from endless battles with Me Marketers—have converged and given rise to the You Marketing revolution.

No longer will consumers be treated like mindless sheep; neither will they be won over by vanity or charisma. Credibility is the new currency. As marketing expert Bryan Kramer explains, consumers want real human connection, the kind they can get only from other people—not from some soulless corporate brand.[3]

Rather than looking at earning this credibility through communication from business to consumer or from business to business, Bryan calls for a human-to-human connection. Your audience is composed of humans, and when you talk to them (whether through online content, daily interactions, or speaking events where you're addressing a large crowd of people), it's critical that you and your brand connect on a human level—on their level.

Just as You Marketing humanizes the consumer, it also humanizes the brand. I mean this quite literally. Your brand isn't a logo or a product; it's a distinct group of people united by a shared vision and values. You Marketing connects the people behind your brand to the people whom your brand benefits.

As a philosophy, You Marketing revolves around a singular question: How can *I* make life better for *you*? Notice that the question is neither "How can I make life better for you so that you'll buy whatever I'm selling?" nor "How can I trick you into believing that I care?" Consumers are too savvy and too wary to be manipulated. The instant you misrepresent yourself or your intentions is the instant you lose all credibility.

That might sound dramatic, but consider your other relationships. Think about one of your closest friends or your partner and imagine that person has lied to, manipulated, or misled you. Doesn't just the thought of that make you feel hurt or betrayed? Remember that feeling because you don't want anyone to ever feel that way about you or your company.

When someone is not genuine or honest with you, that person breaks your trust. And once that's broken, it is very difficult to rebuild. That universal truth applies to your personal and your business relationships. Trust takes significant time and careful effort to build. Act carelessly with it and you'll destroy it.

However, if you can tangibly improve your target audience's quality of life, even in ways that seem minute, they'll begin to think of you as a positive force in their lives.

Do this consistently and your audience will reward you with top-of-mind status.

Building Relationships Through Connectivity

One of the most effective ways to enrich the lives of your target audience is to help fulfill their hunger for relevant, engaging information and insights. Great content—the kind that feeds your audience's appetite—can take nearly endless forms, including insightful think pieces, enlightening how-to videos, and live updates from the front lines of a real-time event.

As the possibilities within digital media become more nuanced and powerful, the demand for instant access is rapidly intensifying.

In fact, the gap between human thought and online action is becoming so minuscule that Google has coined a new term to describe it: the micro-moment.

Most of us experience dozens, if not hundreds or even thousands, of micro-moments every day. It begins with a thought. You are compelled to figure out the how, what, when, where, who, or why of a particular thing. In an instant, without even fully realizing it, you're on your phone or at your laptop, asking the Internet for answers. It doesn't matter that you're not completely conscious of what you're doing; what matters is that you're acting with intent and purpose. According to Google, "Understanding consumer intent and meeting their needs in the moment are the keys to winning more hearts, minds, and dollars."[4]

"Meeting their needs in the moment" is foundational to You Marketing, which makes it a crucial part of achieving top-of-mind status. You can meet your customers' needs only if you know what those needs are. Therefore, you can be effective only if you know how to listen.

Listening to your target audience is *the only way* to know exactly what they want. And because their wants and needs are fluid, you can never stop listening. Whatever methods you use to communicate with your target audience—surveys, data analytics, focus groups, social media engagement—you have to create an open-ended conversation that is as dynamic as your customer base.

As you learn about the needs, wants, and personalities that compose your target audience, certain patterns will start to take shape. Take note of what patterns resonate across your customer base; these are "content triggers," and they are key to establishing a real connection. Use these triggers as a guide in creating and distributing content; they're vital in your journey toward becoming top of mind.

We will delve much deeper into the logistics of effective communication, content creation, and distribution later in the book. For now, remember these three basic steps:

1. Listen to your target audience. What do they value? What's important to them?

2. Craft the way you engage and communicate with this audience around those content triggers.

3. Repeat.

Simple, right?

The School of Inbound

These three steps are also at the heart of inbound marketing. If You Marketing is a philosophy, then inbound is one of its practical applications. Both pursue top of mind as a primary goal.

The rise of inbound is no surprise. None of us wants to be sold to constantly and indiscriminately by stuffy salespeople or obnoxious, intrusive ads. Inbound offers a more intuitive, effective solution to attracting and building an audience.

Later in this book, I'll cover more ways that this basic methodology can be applied to areas beyond marketing; think "inbound recruiting" or "inbound investor relations." But first, let's see what inbound marketing looks like.

According to the experts at HubSpot (a marketing automation tool for inbound marketing), inbound marketers are "creating quality content that pulls people toward your company and product, where they naturally want to be."[5]

Rather than traditional Me Marketing that pushes a company's message onto (often unwilling) consumers, this method of inbound You Marketing draws interested audiences toward your company. Here's how HubSpot maps it out:

Attract. The first step is to attract your target audience to you, and in the digital world, that's very often your website. This means hosting and sharing compelling, engaging content—the most important element of which is your company blog. Getting these audiences to your site can take a few different forms. Maybe it's an article your team published on an external industry publication that links back to relevant content on your site, or maybe your recruiter sent out an e-mail to desirable candidates about recent trends in your industry, enticing them to your company. Whatever combination of tactics you use, your goal is to attract them to you.

Convert. Once prospective customers land on your home page, you need to convert them from visitors into leads by capturing their contact information. Do so by offering access to some form of extra-valuable content (white papers, e-books, etc.) in exchange for their contact information. It works like this: You've gotten your audience's attention well enough to attract them to you and your site. Now it's time to build on that trust by giving them more attractive, valuable resources—not a hard sell. Share your insights first to position yourself as the best resource for them when they're ready to buy.

Close. To turn your leads into customers, nurture the relationship through personalized communication based on how they're interacting with your content and company. That means keeping detailed records in your customer relationship management (CRM) system and tracking your performance. What actions are your leads taking, and how are you responding to them? How could you respond more effectively?

Delight. Finally, transform your customers into promoters of your brand. Unfortunately, it's not uncommon for companies to close a sale and leave the new customer in the hands of the client service team without so much as another word. Sometimes, sales teams lose interest after what they perceive as their portion of the work is complete—that's a bad move. Nothing hurts your new client more than feeling used, like you were only ever interested in the sale.

I know this because when we were a younger company and I was more involved in the sales process, I received a few pieces of feedback that I was engaging and personable right up until the agreement was signed—and then I disappeared.

I know that had to hurt my customers. It hurt me to hear. That was never my intention, but without continued engagement after the deal is done, that's how they'll feel.

We know better today, and we continue to send educational materials to new clients: articles we've written, blog posts, various newsletters, and other tidbits of information after they sign to demonstrate our commitment to helping them even after the first check clears. This education makes your customers better clients; it often eases the transition, prepares them for what's to come, and gives them fuel to share with their own networks down the road.

Don't hesitate to ask for your customers' help promoting your brand with their networks. If this strategy goes well, you'll have an army of brand advocates, ready to connect you with potential future clients and partners—so just ask. I used to feel bad asking for referrals, but if you've done your job well and have maintained that trust you've worked so hard to build, you've earned the ability to ask. (When we asked our clients for referrals and I personally communicated with them for the information, I was blown away by how many of them came through with opportunities for us. If I'd never asked, who knows if they'd have shared that information?)

As you can see, the flow is natural and intuitive—and it works. In its "State of Inbound 2015" report, HubSpot reports that inbound marketing delivers 54 percent more leads than traditional methods and saves companies an average of 13 percent in overall cost per lead.[6] And when companies employ both inbound and traditional outbound methods, inbound campaigns are three times as likely to generate a higher return. Now, take the inbound research from an inbound software company as you will, but I can say that in my own experience, the highest yield comes from the combination of inbound and outbound.

Consider someone who read your article on *Forbes* but didn't click through in your article at that time or someone who saw your company's tweet with your latest update or custom graphic but didn't find her way to your site. An outbound ad campaign that gives these people another opportunity to discover more relevant content could remind them you're there for them—or maybe it will remind them to reach out to you personally.

What about the next time you attend a conference? Instead of shaking hands and focusing on your pitch, you could naturally say, "Hey, let me send you some of the articles I've written that talk about the exact challenges you've mentioned." And if you don't have any articles of your own to send, direct them to other resources on your website or company social media accounts that address their needs. You can connect people to the resources they need and position yourself as someone they can trust without having authored every piece of content yourself (although it certainly helps to have a few pieces of your own).

You can apply this basic methodology to every way you communicate with your audience. Whatever specific tactics you use to practice this, your goal should always be to educate and provide value first and close later.

On Top of Many Minds

Up to this point, I've focused primarily on You Marketing as a way to build connections with your audience. And indeed, the data on inbound and the rise of content marketing are indisputable evidence of the benefits of achieving top-of-mind status within your customer base. But what if your target audience isn't your actual customer?

The same principles are just as powerful when applied to any aspect of your business in which success depends on flourishing human relationships. I was recently at a CMO dinner hosted by my friend Pete Krainik. Pete asked the group how we felt about vendors, and angry murmurs rippled around the table.

CMOs are influential people who have the power to make major decisions; one decision could mean millions of dollars spent somewhere else instead of with your company. (Believe me, I've seen it happen, and it sucks when you can't save that situation because you haven't built up enough trust.)

If we take my fellow diners as a representative sample, then the state of CMO-vendor affairs is grim. Fortunately, inbound and You Marketing concepts offer a hopeful way forward for vendors to build trust with this critical audience.

According to research by Forrester, buyers are often between 70 and 90 percent of the way through the sales process before they ever engage a vendor.[7] That means your buyers are out there researching their problems and trying to identify potential solutions—and they're learning about the most trustworthy companies that can help. You have to do everything you can to ensure they're finding the right information to educate, engage, and attract them to you before you hop on a call.

I don't know a single person who starts his buying process by calling each salesperson he knows from all the companies he can think of and asking those salespeople how they can help him. That's ridiculous. He'd start by searching online to learn more about his specific problem and what people have to say about it to arm himself with as much information as possible before ever talking to someone about buying solutions.

Now consider that it takes between 7 and 13 "touches," or interactions with your brand, for a lead to become sales-ready.[8] By providing relevant, accessible content, you're ensuring your audience has ample opportunity for the kind of interaction that leads them to your company.

And when you do finally engage a lead in a sales capacity (in the remaining 20 or 30 percent of their journey), that lead will already feel a strong human connection to the people behind your brand because he's interacted with you up to a dozen times already. He's asked and answered many of his own questions by searching online, and because your brand's content helped him during his journey, yours is the brand he'll turn to when it is time to engage a salesperson. That's how you achieve the best results and truly build relationships with the people who can help you succeed.

The same is true for recruiting. In 2015, CareerBuilder found that more than three out of four employed workers are actively seeking new job opportunities. That's a process that consists of some significant homework—the average candidate will consult 16 total resources throughout her job search.[9]

CareerBuilder calls it the "candidate-powered economy," which should strike a healthy bit of fear in the hearts of HR recruiters—the same kind of fear that initially struck salespeople when they realized their audiences were powering the conversations, too. So what does it take to entice talent from this hypermobile, well-researched talent pool?

Interestingly, 77 percent of candidates would lower their salary expectations if an employer created a great impression before or during the hiring process. Even more compelling is that 83 percent would do the same to work with a company that has a reputation as a great employer.

Therefore, it's not enough to run the happiest, most fulfilling workplace in the world—you also have to facilitate an emotional connection between your company and the talent pool. And anything you do to communicate that can build a strong connection. From current and former employee reviews and workplace awards to a blog series on your company culture and an "About" page that highlights a positive environment, the content that's out there about your company will affect the kinds of emotional connections prospective candidates form with you before ever walking into their first interview.

Be warned, however, that talent will judge the quality of external communications, including your content, as a reflection of your quality as an employer. Pump out garbage, and you'll come off as a terrible place to work. But craft content that is aimed directly at your ideal candidate—meaning that it's relevant, compelling, and distributed through the right channels—and you'll create an enticing glimpse into your culture, values, and vision. In time, you'll find yourself on top of the minds of the people you want working with you.

It's easy to see that You Marketing and inbound principles can get you top of mind with any target audience, from consumers and talent to investors, partners, and media relations. In fact, you can apply these concepts to any relationship—even those outside your business life.

Let's return to the three basic steps of the top-of-mind approach: Listen to your target audience; engage and communicate with them in ways they find helpful and meaningful; and repeat. Listen, engage, and repeat.

Now, I'm no couples counselor, so take this advice with a grain of salt: if you are constantly listening to and communicating with your partner, you're doing it right. The same is true with family and friends.

That's not to say that you should approach your personal and business relationships in entirely the same way all the time. You absolutely should not. My point is that when you're authentic, helpful, and respectful in all of your relationships, good things fall into place.

Think about how you interact with people, both personally and professionally, and make it a habit to listen attentively, communicate and engage thoughtfully with them, and be consistent in your efforts.

Listen. Engage. Repeat.

2

WHAT CONSUMERS ARE LOOKING FOR IN BRANDS THEY TRUST

It wasn't long ago that my company, Influence & Co., was a young startup. Those early days were a sleepless roller coaster of excitement and frustration. As a new entrepreneur, I remember being blindsided by the emotional intensity of it all. Thinking back, one memory sticks out as both a little traumatic and incredibly formative.

We were struggling to make things work as a company. It was getting to me pretty bad, and I started to doubt not only the company but myself and my abilities, too.

I was attending a networking session at one of my first conferences. I didn't know a single person there. However, with my background in sales and experience in real estate, I thought I'd still have shot at schmoozing my way to some success.

But something wasn't working. I was getting stonewalled—not just by one or two people but by everyone. I couldn't connect for the life of me. The sense of not being able to get through to a single person was overwhelming.

All of a sudden, I felt the same defeated feeling you might have experienced in your middle school gym class playing dodgeball, when the team captains are down to two remaining options: you and another kid. You're hoping the captain calls your name so you're not left standing there alone and embarrassed, but he calls on the other kid instead. You immediately feel like an outcast, and you give up before the game even starts.

That's how I felt.

Once I left the event, I called my wife. After a minute of doing my best to put a positive spin on what I'd just experienced, I broke down. I remember talking to her with tears in my eyes, struggling to be honest about how things weren't going well. We had poured all of our energy and emotion into this company, only to discover that we'd launched in an industry devoid of opportunity. It was a hopeless, desperate feeling.

Now when I think about that phone call, I cringe a bit. Embarrassing, humiliating, kind of dramatic—not exactly feelings I like to relive. But I also feel a sense of gratitude. As awful as it was, that experience inspired me to look at opportunity from a completely different perspective.

Why couldn't I connect? Why was everyone so guarded? The answer was simple: because nobody trusted me. No one was even familiar with me. It wasn't enough to be charming. I had walked into a roomful of strangers (most of whom already knew one another and had done business together) with nothing to show that I was worthy of their trust. I was just another random guy making a cold pitch—the human equivalent of a pop-up ad.

As I thought more about it, I realized that my despair was misplaced. Our industry wasn't some barren, opportunityless wasteland; there were too many success stories for that to be the case.

The truth was that the field was brimming with endless opportunity—but all of it was locked up behind a giant wall of distrust.

I learned that these walls of distrust—or trust barriers—exist everywhere. No matter what field or niche or position level or company size, trust barriers exist. And they're the biggest factors that prevent you from building relationships with the audiences you're trying to reach.

My whole founding team at Influence & Co. dealt with similar situations, too. Brent Beshore, the CEO of our holding company, adventur.es, faced barriers when he had to earn the trust of the new companies he was prepared to invest in. My cofounder, Kelsey Meyer, struggled to be taken seriously as a young entrepreneur. Although she was probably brighter than most people 15 years her senior, she was still fresh out of college.

When I talked to a friend of mine about the struggles he faced as an experienced salesperson switching industries, he told me about his troubles building a solid client list. Even though he had experience and knew what he was doing, no one in this new industry knew that about him. They weren't familiar with him at all.

My brother had the same problem: He started a law practice and was trying to attract the right partners. No one was beating down his office door demanding to work with him. He had to build trust with his audience before he could get anywhere.

All this is to say that my situation at this conference was not unique. Everyone deals with trust barriers, not just my fellow marketing, branding, and PR peers.

After we'd come to this revelation and while we were still scrambling to survive the launch stage, we began contemplating a set of questions that were as complex as they were simple:

What is trust?

What does it mean to be trustworthy?

Why do people trust each other?

Understanding Trust

My first lesson was to stop thinking about trust as if it were an inanimate object that either exists or does not.

Trust is a living, breathing, emotional bond that connects people to one another. It's intimate, personal, and powerful. In a world where it seems like everyone is out to pitch, scam, or screw you, it is also a rare and precious commodity.

Trust manifests itself on a spectrum. The degree to which you trust someone determines how far out you'll stick your neck for her. Therefore, to overcome barriers of distrust, it's not enough just to be a trustworthy person—you have to be a person who creates trust.

Think of it like a campfire. To be trustworthy is to have your kindling, wood, tinder, and matches all set up and ready to go. But in the immortal words of rock icon and park ranger Bruce Springsteen, you can't start a fire without a spark.

As you'll see, there are no shortcuts to gaining someone's trust. It takes time to create an emotional bond and energy to bring it to life. If you don't make a long-term commitment to keeping the fire going, it will quickly burn out.

Trust Plus Consistency Equals Opportunity

The deeper I delved into my exploration of trust, the clearer its relationship to opportunity became.

Think of the people you trust most in the world. (For me, they are my wife and mother: two people who consistently help, educate, challenge, and make me better in every way.)

How long did it take you to picture their faces? One second? Maybe two? And when was the last time you thought of these people? I'm going to guess that it hasn't been longer than a week or two. Now make a mental list of the things you'd absolutely never ever do for these people if they were to ask you for help. Pretty short list, isn't it?

When you trust someone completely, you place that person directly at the topmost point of your mind. And so long as you trust that person, he or she will stay there. You'll do whatever you can for him or her, seeking out and creating opportunities to make life better for him or her.

This can all be distilled into a simple formula, shown in Figure 2.1. In other words, if you can consistently generate and sustain trust, you can create your own opportunity.

Figure 2.1 **Formula for Creating Opportunity**

TRUST   CONSISTENCY   OPPORTUNITY

Now I'm not saying you can be everyone's wife or mother. (That's just weird.) What you can do is hit enough trust touch points that you earn a place at the top of people's minds so you're the first person they think of when it's time to make a decision. Think of it as a trust equity meter: each touch point helps you get another share of trust equity, and you'll become a larger holder of their trust.

When someone is looking to hire an attorney or work with a designer for her company's website or developing partnerships for his next opportunity, the person who's built trust, hit enough touch points, and earned top-of-mind status will get the first call.

On the personal side, it could be that a friend of yours has an extra ticket to the Grammys and is looking for someone to go with. You want your name to be the first one that comes to mind. (I saw this happen. I knew someone who had an extra ticket to the Grammys, and you know what? The person who got the first call was one who had recently helped this friend move some furniture into his house. See? This mindset can apply to more than strictly professional opportunities.)

It may sound intuitive (it is), and it may sound like alchemy (it's not). Either way, this formula was the culmination of my studies in trust, and it hit me like a divine revelation. Since making it the central pillar of our business philosophy, Influence & Co. has grown substantially: we've had a revenue growth of 5,000 percent, earned a place on the *Forbes* "Most Promising Companies in America" list, received recognition by the United Nations with an Empact Award for Best Marketing and Advertising Company, and recently ranked on the Inc. 500. More important than accolades, though, is that we're surrounded by constant opportunities for growth.

But it's easy to talk about how wonderful and important trust is in business and in life. The real question is, How do you make it happen?

Touch Points for Creating Trust

Trying to force another human being to trust you is both manipulative and counterproductive. You can't make someone feel an emotion; you can only create the conditions for that emotion to emerge organically.

The following touch points are ways to create these conditions. Because we're dealing with complex human emotions, don't think of this as a rigid checklist that will guarantee a specific set of results. Instead, think of it as a fluid set of guidelines for carrying yourself in a way that invites people to trust you.

What follows is an overview; we'll delve deeper into each touch point later in the book.

Authenticity

You cannot trust what you don't believe to be real. And yet so many of us contort ourselves into some premade mold of what we think we're supposed to be. The introverted entrepreneur strains to be the life of the party, and the fun-loving CEO forces a constant scowl to come off as a person of seriousness.

What is true in your personal life is just as true in your professional one: bullshit derails relationships. When you pretend, not only are you putting distance between yourself and your next opportunity, you're making yourself miserable as well.

When I was younger, I used to think it was cool to call my friends and share (or exaggerate) my successes. I felt a pressure to impress others, and as I got older, I realized I was actually hurting my relationships with my closest friends. I was acting like someone I wasn't, and they could see right through it.

In 2014, Target CMO Jeff Jones published a post on LinkedIn titled "The Truth Hurts."[1] The post came as Target was trying to rebuild after the news of a massive data breach, compounded by the sudden resignation of its CEO in the fallout. Rather than trying to spin the terrible news, Jones was completely up front—not only about the impact of the crisis on the business but also about the emotional toll it was taking on the team and on himself.

Jones's authenticity inspired me. I began to write more openly about the self-doubt I experience about my writing skills (a nerve-racking prospect for the head of a content marketing company). These articles were exercises in authenticity.

The response was tremendous (and unexpected). Needless to say, given what my company does, this created quite a few new opportunities for us. The connections this sort of authenticity helped forge have been as vital for our business as they have been for my personal growth.

Take a minute to evaluate your own authenticity. You're reading a book. Nobody's judging you. Be honest with yourself here.

Years ago, if I had spent time thinking about my own authenticity and asking myself if I was truly authentic, it would have been a brief exercise in self-awareness. The answer would have been "Absolutely not." It's not like I was actively trying to be inauthentic, but as I said, I used to feel a constant pressure to impress others. And that sort of motivation doesn't lend itself very well to developing or practicing authenticity.

Since then, I've continued to make a conscious effort to challenge myself to become better, and I've been fortunate enough to surround myself with people who aren't afraid to call me out when I need it. When you've got good intentions and you're trying to become the best version of yourself, authenticity extends naturally from those efforts.

I'll leave you with this on authenticity: There are certain things to which people are naturally drawn, things we've got a sense for, and I firmly believe that authenticity is one of them. My three-year-old daughter loves the movie *Aladdin* so much that she wants to watch it together basically every night.

Now, if you've ever seen *Aladdin*, you know that one of his three wishes is to become a prince so that he can impress Princess Jasmine. When she starts getting suspicious of him, the Genie advises Aladdin to just drop the act and tell her the truth already, later turning into a bee and whispering "Bee yourself" into Aladdin's ear.

This is the part where my daughter gets so frustrated (and it's kind of amazing to watch). She throws a fit every time and says, "Daddy, why is Aladdin being like this?" My three-year-old can tell when something isn't authentic, and I don't think that ability goes away as we get older. In fact, I think we get better at sensing it. We become more skeptical and, therefore, even more attracted to authentic relationships (and brands).

Helping Others

If you're still skeptical about whether it's possible to create opportunity for yourself, try doing it for someone else. It might sound counterintuitive, but one of the best ways to help yourself is to help others.

It's easy: each time you speak to someone, simply close the conversation by asking, "How can I be helpful to you?"

Being this direct will give you insight into the barriers that stand between this person and his goals—and how you can help dismantle those barriers. Sometimes doing so is easy and all you have to do is shoot off a quick e-mail or make a phone call to connect people to the resources that will help them meet their goals.

Recently, a member of my publications team was at a conference on the West Coast that was hosted by a particular media outlet. We were using Slack to catch up, and I asked if there was anything I could do to help her out. She was struggling to set up a meeting with this media outlet, and it turned out that I knew the SVP of that company. With an e-mail that took me a total of 30 seconds to write, I reached out to him, and he provided my team member with exactly what she needed—and we made a new business opportunity happen. My employee was so grateful. I could tell that something as simple as an e-mail went a long way to building more trust between us.

If it weren't for people introducing me to their strategic contacts, providing constructive feedback on my pitches, and sharing valuable industry insight, Influence & Co. would certainly not be where it is today. Minor though they may seem individually, these acts of helpfulness add up and have determined the course of my business and my life. I've never forgotten the people behind them.

More cynical readers might accuse me of advocating bribery. Not true. A favor with strings attached may achieve some sort of immediate quid pro quo, but it has no lasting power. It's far more effective to help others without expecting anything in return. Most people will feel deep appreciation, and appreciation is a ladder to top-of-mind position. When helping others becomes the framework through which you interact with the world, you'll find yourself at the top of many minds.

Likability

I tend to think of myself as somewhat of a likable person. I grew up in the Midwest, after all, which is like coming of age in a likability boot camp—or so I thought. Then I read Jeff Haden's article "How to Be Exceptionally Likable: 11 Things the Most Charming People Always Do,"[2] and I realized I had some major work to do.

Likability matters. It's hard to trust someone you don't like. Because we are passionate, high-energy people, this is something that many entrepreneurs and executives struggle with, as the intensity of our passion can easily rub others the wrong way. It's necessary to find a balance between intensity and accessibility, one that neither suppresses nor sacrifices authenticity.

Finding that balance starts with understanding yourself and your personality and exactly what kind of "likable" you want to be. Jeff Haden offers some great advice, and later, we'll go into more depth about applying his list of advice to your unique brand of likability. It takes work, but investing in your likability will pay off in trust.

Familiarity

Familiarity is the other side of the likability coin—it evokes a sense of closeness, a feeling of genuine connection. Familiarity emerges at its purest in face-to-face conversation.

Imagine yourself at one of those networking sessions where everyone you talk to is looking slightly beyond your left ear, scanning the room for someone more important. After a few of these interactions, you meet someone who is actually curious—not only about your business idea but about you as a person. The questions are real without being intrusive. Where did you grow up? Where do you get your ideas? What do you love about what you do? Just imagine how this person would stand out from the rest.

I had an experience like this recently. I was at St. Mary's University, waiting around to address students at their graduation ceremony.

With some time on my hands, I approached the organizer and struck up a conversation. Within minutes we made the surprising discovery that we had grown up three blocks away from each other. Three blocks.

The sense of familiarity I feel with him now is as strong as if I'd known him for years. Had one of us looked slightly past the other to find someone else or stuck to superficial small talk, we would still be strangers. Cultivating a sense of genuine curiosity and learning to ask the right questions will help build familiarity with others and transform you from random outsider to trusted insider.

Brand and Thought Leadership

If you treat your brand as an afterthought, you're simply fortifying the barriers between yourself and opportunity creation. A vibrant, flourishing brand is one of your most powerful tools in creating trust and opportunity.

Take a look at Tesla. If you're not a luxury electric vehicle industry insider, you may not know much about the inner workings of the company. Chances are, however, that you're familiar with Elon Musk's reputation as rocket scientist/climate activist/genius innovator— or, as blogger Tim Urban calls him, the "world's raddest man."[3]

Perhaps you're one of Musk's millions of Twitter followers, or maybe you just notice when he's quoted in an article on tech, which is all of them. The benefits Musk reaps from his stellar brand extend to his companies, too.

Now compare Musk to my friend Dave Kerpen. Unlike Musk, Dave isn't a billionaire celebrity (though he is a pretty rad guy). But that hasn't stopped Dave from becoming one of the most respected thought leaders in the field of digital marketing. To achieve and sustain this position, Dave maintains an impeccable personal brand— he publishes some of the most insightful content across the most relevant platforms, engages his audience in meaningful, personal conversations, and comes off as the great guy he really is. The success of Dave's brand has been a huge asset to the success of Likeable Local, as well as Likeable Media—and will be an asset to any company he's involved with in the future.

It is vital that you invest in executive branding—not just your own but your entire team's. Each of your team members is a potential thought leader; the more thought leaders represent your brand, the more trust you generate with more audiences who can relate to you.

Content Triggers

Have you ever read an article that feels like it was written especially for you? Maybe it answers a specific question you've had on your mind for a while or it gives you some piece of advice that seems tailor-made to your life situation. When this happens, it creates a sense of connection to the author that makes you want to read everything she's ever written and anything she'll ever write.

Content triggers help foster this connection between you and your audience. As we talked about in Chapter 1, these triggers are the patterns that emerge when you listen to the demands of your target audience. The question to ask should sound pretty familiar to you: "How can I be helpful to you?"

When we started listening, really listening, to our audience, we learned that many executives who were enthusiastic about investing in content marketing were getting insurmountable pushback from their CFOs. So we began crafting content around this content trigger, publishing articles like "4 C-Suite Objections to Content Marketing and How to Overcome Them."[4] By speaking directly to the needs of our target audience, we were able to gain their trust.

Education

Education is the most important trust point because knowledge is power. When you educate people, you are empowering them.

All of the previous touch points fall under the umbrella of education in one way or another. One of the most effective and easily scalable ways to unify these practices is through high-quality digital content.

Content's potential as an educational tool is limitless. Use it to share whatever knowledge you have that others will find valuable—industry insight, best practices, experiential learnings—and they will reward you with trust.

If this all seems like a lot to take in, don't worry. In the following chapters, we'll explore tactics for transforming these trust touch points into habits. Once these strategies become second nature, everything you do will generate trust and get you closer to being top of mind.

3

BUILDING RELATIONSHIPS
BY HELPING OTHERS

YOU INTERACT WITH PEOPLE in business every day, and you can handle these interactions in one of two ways.

1. You are strictly business-focused and actively think about what you can do to develop these interactions into relationships that serve your goals on your terms.

2. You're more natural about your approach and care about other people for who they are, not what they can do for you.

I prefer the second option, and not just because I know it's more effective; it also preserves my mental health and makes my life more enjoyable. Thinking about life and people like they're pieces of a puzzle that exist to help me achieve my goals would be exhausting, and it'd make me feel terrible. Caring about people is more natural, and building mutually beneficial relationships based on that is, well, mutually beneficial. It just makes sense.

About three years ago, I met Scott Gerber, a man who so completely personifies the superconnector archetype that Shane Snow describes him as "the Pandora of Gen-Y networking."[1]

As the founder of the Young Entrepreneur Council (YEC) and CommunityCo, two professional communities, Scott plays gatekeeper to some of the most valuable networks in our industry. I knew that if I could build a good relationship with him and persuade him to work with Influence & Co., our partnership would be mutually beneficial.

Now, when you know that a partnership would be good for both of you, it can be hard not to take the first approach I outlined above—the business-first, swing-for-the-fences technique.

However, instead of pushing for an official partnership right away, we let a personal relationship emerge organically. After our meeting, we began helping each other out in whatever ways we could. We shared feedback on each other's projects and made strategic introductions whenever the opportunity arose. In other words, we had each other's backs.

Since then, our relationship has flourished. As Scott became a close and trusted friend, YEC became a close and trusted ally. We would do almost anything to help Scott and YEC succeed, and that commitment is mutual. This is a fulfilling relationship that pays off in trust, shared resources, and brand equity. As a result, the business relationship has become extremely strong, surviving hiccups that probably would have put an end to a partnership if the relationship wasn't there.

Good things happen when you help people out rather than treating them as extensions of your business plan. For one thing, helping others tends to make you feel pretty good about life. Your network becomes a group of people you like and trust. Your interactions become friendly, genuine, and infused with humanity. That's why helpful people often radiate a sense of confidence and gratitude.

But the benefits aren't only emotional. It may seem counterintuitive, but one of the most effective ways to develop a competitive business advantage—even if you're operating in a cutthroat industry—is to be helpful to others. And I'm not talking about doling out Frank Underwood–style quid pro quo favors; I'm talking about being a kind, supportive person without expecting anything in return.

My friend Brittany Hodak, CEO of ZinePak, once said in a Startup Weekend speech, "Don't be intimidated by hard-to-get relationships. At each one of these brands or organizations, there are people behind it, and all you need is a solid relationship with one to create a spark." She was referring to her strong partnership with Walmart and obtaining that partnership as a startup.

Think about the industry leader you admire most. He or she is most likely a knowledgeable, well-connected, credible person who faces few industry barriers. And though some leaders might blather on about climbing the ladder through sheer force of will alone, most are eager to acknowledge the helpful people who have been invaluable to their success.

I remember one of our first clients, Drew McLellan, owner of Agency Management Institute, who helped make us a stronger company when we honestly didn't know what we were doing. He and his feedback helped us become the company we are today; he's come to me since then to ask for help because he knows I'll be there for him. Now, Drew isn't my best friend or anything, but we've formed a bond that continues to be mutually beneficial. Without these kinds of helpful people and mutually beneficial relationships in life, who knows where we'd be.

By helping your partners, business leads, clients, and other industry connections, you not only win their gratitude, you also position yourself as a person with knowledge, resources, and credibility—the makings of an industry leader. What's more, when you practice helpfulness as a leader, you inspire your team to do the same. And companies known for their amiability and expertise aren't just profitable; they're beloved.

But what if you're not an inherently altruistic person? Just like mindfulness, helpfulness is a practice that you can learn and develop so that it becomes second nature. But you can't treat it as some fluffy afterthought; helpfulness requires authenticity, consistency, and intention. And as this chapter progresses, you'll learn more about the techniques for incorporating helpfulness into everything that you and your team do.

If the notion of a corporate culture steeped in altruism sounds like a stretch, consider this: A couple years ago, Influence & Co. hired Matt Kamp, a guy fresh out of college with very little sales experience whose sole responsibility was to help out the people in our network—not only to help those we would see the highest returns from but to genuinely offer our resources, relationships, knowledge, and so on to the people in our network who could use them, just for the sake of being helpful to them.

He has a touch point system in place to regularly connect with and lend a helping hand based on each contact's needs, whether through press opportunities, referrals, or simply relevant information. As a result, Matt—who was not initially even a member of our sales team—has become one of our leading sales performers. (It doesn't hurt that he's so naturally likable, either. His personality is a perfect match for this type of role.)

In addition to his sales performance, hiring Matt as our "director of helpfulness" has been an incredibly powerful way to build thriving relationships across our growing network. As a result, we've gained a massive community of brand advocates who are constantly promoting Influence & Co. and sending referrals our way. In fact, partner referrals accounted for our largest lead source for new revenue in 2015. Our helpfulness practice positions us at the top of countless minds, providing us actionable, profitable opportunities every day.

So how can you do the same?

Putting Helpfulness into Practice

When we're talking about how to help others, there are no universal formulas or absolute rules to follow. Helpfulness is not a science; it's a personal, intimate practice. It's up to you to define, shape, and develop your practice in a way that is authentic to you.

That said, there are so many potential ways to "do" helpfulness that the prospect of incorporating it into your professional life may seem overwhelming. Therefore, it's worth mapping out some broad guidelines for how you can easily and effectively make life better for the people in your network—and identifying the tools to help you execute those guidelines.

As you read this chapter (and those that follow), you'll notice references to the Resource Library at the back of this book that contains lists of tools, software, and more designed to help you execute your top-of-mind mindset. As comprehensive as I've tried to be, resources like these change all the time, so I've created an e-mail address (topofmindhelp@gmail.com) that you can use to reach me or someone on my team if you're looking for more specific information or if you have questions in the course of your research.[2]

As you go through the following list of best helpfulness practices, you'll notice that none of them requires you to spend any money (except possibly "give gifts," but even with this one, you don't have to spend much at all). In fact, most can be done with just a quick e-mail, phone call, or friendly conversation.

Note that these guidelines are based on my own experience and personality. Some of these will work for you; others may not. Feel free to use these as a foundation for your practice and interpret them however you see fit. The CRM systems such as Contactually, SalesforceIQ, and others listed in the Resource Library at the end of this book can help.

Share Knowledge

To share your knowledge of the world and your experience within it is to share your most valuable asset. When you offer someone useful information, you're providing a very real form of currency. This currency could come in the form of an industry tip, an in-depth analysis, or personal wisdom. Whatever the form, helpful knowledge enriches people's lives.

I like to think of it this way: storytelling and sharing knowledge is a big part of our humanity, and we wouldn't be where we are today without it. Imagine if our ancestors never told stories or if Einstein or Ford never shared their ideas with anyone else.

I make it a point to take the time to share my knowledge when someone asks. This isn't to say that I think my knowledge is necessarily as revolutionary as Einstein's—but there just might be a nugget of information in my stories that helps someone or resonates so strongly with people that they go on to bring their own revolutionary ideas to life. Sharing my knowledge and experiences for a few minutes could save them days or weeks (or even years) of wasted time and help them bring opportunity to themselves, too.

Unfortunately, as much as I love them, in-person conversations aren't scalable. I can't talk and share stories with everyone in person, so this leads us to the obvious solution of digital content. And I'm not the only one to use content to share knowledge.

Let me walk you through an example of what I like to call a "knowledge chain."

Labor laws in the United States have recently changed, and an attorney with a firm we've used in the past, Armstrong Teasdale, sent some members of my team a few articles and other pieces of content about the changes and what to look out for. He didn't bill us for that service. He was just looking out for us and knew that part of being a good service provider is educating your clients throughout the process.

My HR director is a rock star and pored through all this new information not only so she could be knowledgeable herself but also so she could teach me. Not long after we'd gone through the changes together, I spoke with Patrick Ambron, CEO of BrandYourself and a good friend of ours. Being the creative, hardworking entrepreneur he is, he'd kept his head down on several projects and wasn't in the loop when it came to the details of the new laws. So I let him know.

He was very thankful, and all I did was share some information with him that I thought he would find valuable. Was that difficult for me to do? No. All I did was what humans have done forever: learn something new and share it with others. And at each link in this knowledge chain—from an attorney to my HR director to me to a fellow entrepreneur—trust was strengthened.

We couldn't each meet with one another in person to discuss these updates, and there's no way that any of the others who've been affected by this shared knowledge could possibly join these meetings either. That's where thought leadership content comes in. Through articles, digital content, social communication, speaking engagements, and the like, you can share insights with huge audiences at once. Consistently deliver useful knowledge to your target audience, and you'll always be top of mind.

Connect People with What They Value

If you're a new parent, you're familiar with the concept of "unhelpful help." You're at a dinner with relatives and you mention that your baby hasn't been sleeping through the night. There's a split second of silence. Your mom's ears perk up, your uncle cocks his head, your sister inhales deeply, and all at once, every person in your family is blasting you with advice that you never asked for.

In business, offering unhelpful help can cost you credibility and weaken your relationships. It can make you seem out-of-touch at best and manipulative at worst, as if you're trying to curry favor but aren't very good at it.

You can help a person only if you know what kind of help she would find valuable. So rather than guessing, come right out and ask.

When I meet someone, I end the conversation by asking, "So how can I be helpful to you moving forward?" and give him an example of what I think would be helpful, such as, "If I run into this type of person, would an intro be valuable?" The question itself is a thoughtful gesture, and it helps forge a bond that will serve as the foundation of a relationship. I log the answer on a spreadsheet so that I can stay on top of connecting the people in my network to what they find valuable, much as our director of helpfulness does.

People know what they need, and when you deliver on those needs, you'll earn gratitude, respect, and top-of-mind status.

Share Resources

You're likely invested in a ton of diverse resources, from core assets such as talent and infrastructure to luxury items such as season tickets for your favorite sports team. At any given moment, a percentage of these resources are going unused.

Think about how you could mobilize your idle assets in creative ways to help your contacts. One of your partners is scrambling to launch a new website; if your star developer is between projects, could she lend a hand? A client needs a place to host a community service event over the weekend; how about your office? Or what about those season tickets? Surely someone in your network would appreciate a night at the stadium.

Something my team and I realized we could share with our contacts is our software. In the last year, we've developed a custom software that helps us with everything from managing content contributors and projects to streamlining communication and tracking analytics for ourselves and our clients.

We realized that these tools gave us great insight into information that our media and publication relationships could benefit from. So we shared it with them. And so far, it's helped their staff members save time and their publications run more efficiently.

In return, we've built stronger, more trusting relationships with our publication contacts—which puts us top of mind for them and puts us in a position to streamline the service side of our business. Anytime you've got something of value, think about who in your network might benefit from it and how you can share it to strengthen your relationship with those people.

You can extend this sharing philosophy to any asset or any relationship. (Just be sure that you are respectful of your time, capacity, and desires when offering help to others).

Once, my neighbor saw me cutting down a tree in my yard with a handsaw. Noticing my struggle, he came over, handed me his electric saw, and said, "Hey, bud, this will save you about half the time, and you can have a beer with me with the time I saved you." He instantly became my favorite neighbor; now we're watching each other's houses when the other is out of town and taking out each other's dogs. And it all started when he offered to help me that day in my yard by sharing his resources.

What resources do you or your company have that you can share?

Make People Aware of Opportunities

Even if you're not invested in any physical assets, you're still capable of helping people fulfill pressing needs. Whenever you hear of an opportunity—whether in the form of a potential partnership, an exciting event, or a journalist looking for industry contacts—you have a shareable resource. Connecting the people in your network to these strategic opportunities generates trust and goodwill.

At the beginning of each year, my team combs through every potential conference in business leadership, entrepreneurship, and marketing to see what events would be valuable for us to attend. No joke, as we were sitting together working through our lists, I received a direct message on Twitter from a contact at *Time* who, as it turned out, had just finished planning out her own conferences to attend.

In her message, she included her list and said, "Hey, I know you guys look into stuff like this. I hope it helps." The timing could not have been more perfect, and it helped us capitalize on a few opportunities we wouldn't have known about without her help.

To scale this idea of making contacts aware of opportunities, occasionally I like to publish lists in my columns in *Forbes* or *Inc.* (I know some people love to hate listicles, but they can be extremely valuable if you do them right.) I now write lists of top conferences, industry trends, and blog and publication lists to help make my audience aware of opportunities, and my latest two have been a couple of my most successful articles—not just in views but also in people letting me know how helpful they found it.

On top of that, I've also heard from conference organizers that these lists have attracted thousands of people to their events. It's a win for everyone involved. Was it difficult? No; all I did was make people aware of these events. Was it scalable? Absolutely. Between the two articles, these lists have generated a couple hundred thousand views.

But maybe you don't have an outlet like that to broadcast your message and make so many people aware of opportunities at once. That's totally fine—you don't need extensive lists of resources or access to major publications to make someone aware of potential opportunity.

I had the chance to address an audience at an event recently, and afterward, someone who'd seen me speak sent me an e-mail letting me know of a company he thought could use Influence & Co.'s services. He'd heard someone at lunch talk about how his company just increased its budgets in thought leadership, content marketing, and PR and saw them as huge strategic initiatives in the near future. Talk about a dream client for Influence & Co.

All he said in his e-mail was that this company was looking for services that mine specializes in, and he thought there was a big opportunity there. This guy didn't have to do any of that for me, but he went out of his way to make me aware of a potential client or partner. Since then, I've probably sent him 10 clients. I don't believe for a minute that he gave me the heads-up so that I'd return the favor, but it sure was an effective way to build trust with me.

Whenever possible, go further than simply sharing information and make personal introductions. Remember, a well-timed opportunity can change someone's life. And introductions are often repaid in kind: I've seen that more than 50 percent of the people for whom I make introductions will do the same for me within a year.

Offer Transparent Feedback

I don't love being criticized. However, if it's between constructive criticism and a meaningless ego stroke, I'll take the former in a heartbeat.

Transparent feedback is a gift. When you offer it to someone, you're saying, "I take you seriously, and I want to help you succeed." Of course, you actually have to mean it—if you don't really want the person to do well, any feedback you provide will be tinged with spite. Although it's technically possible to be helpful and spiteful at the same time, just choose one; it'll be less confusing.

I'm probably not alone in thinking of Simon Cowell when it comes to straightforward feedback. When my wife and I used to watch *American Idol*, I always wondered why he was so popular. (Honestly, he seemed like a big asshole to me.) The more I watched, the clearer it became to me that he was actually offering straightforward, transparent feedback. And more important, I got the feeling that he did it with the intent to help the person on the receiving end of that feedback, not just to be an ass.

And that's exactly where that fine line is: if the way you're delivering feedback doesn't seem like it was meant to be helpful—in other words, if you're just criticizing or being an ass—it's going to be misinterpreted. So although what you say is important, how you say it carries a lot of weight, too.

For example, one of my company's new customers recently contacted me directly to let me know that another client of ours, who had referred him, had a terrible experience with our service. He was matter-of-fact in explaining the situation, gave us a suggestion for what to do about it, and ended by saying that all he wanted was to make sure we were aware of that experience.

Without this new customer coming to me and letting me know, we probably wouldn't have had any idea what was going on. But after some digging and extra communication, we learned it was all a misunderstanding with our original client, and we addressed what we could to move forward in a healthy way. Not only did this new customer's feedback help us clarify the situation, it made us a stronger company.

That's the power of transparent feedback. It can help you become a better person, team member, and company leader, and it can make your company stronger than before. I value that opportunity, so I've made it a personal habit to tell people the honest truth when they ask for feedback. As much as I might want to softball it, I don't let myself. This habit doesn't give me license to be rude or disrespectful—it just means I do my best to deliver the pure and simple truth.

Not long ago, I was at a conference watching a keynote delivered by a big industry personality. When the speaker finished, a crowd formed to shout praises at him for delivering such a wonderful speech. But the truth was, it hadn't been a great speech—he had simply recounted his company's victories without teaching us, the audience, anything. Much to the discomfort of the adoring crowd, I informed the emperor that he wasn't wearing any clothes. He was taken aback, but because I was transparent in my criticism, he listened.

After the event, he texted me to invite me to a birthday party of one of the most well-known leaders in our industry. Because I was honest, I was helpful. And because I was helpful, I was remembered.

The bond that this created has led to both a professional relationship and a personal friendship.

I still remember the person who first offered constructive criticism on one of my earliest articles about being careful with ego in writing. He said, "Remember, writing isn't all about you. It's about a connection to the reader, so do everything you can to keep that connection. And don't do anything to risk it." I think of him with gratitude every time I publish. Always practice transparent feedback; it is a powerful way to achieve top-of-mind status.

Become a Brand Advocate

Next to the love I feel for my family and friends, there is no greater love than what I feel for our brand advocates. Seriously, the sense of affection I feel when I hear someone not on payroll talking up our company can be overwhelming.

When you stand up for someone else's brand, you are performing one of the most fundamentally helpful services imaginable. In today's You Marketing economy, credible endorsements are priceless. Even micro-influencers, those with fewer than 100,000 social media followers, can greatly affect a buyer's decision. More than 80 percent of people are likely to follow the recommendation of a micro-influencer they trust.[3] Advocates generate trust, forge connections, and bolster brand equity in ways that nothing else can.

One of Influence & Co.'s big brand advocates is the CEO of Hawke Media, Erik Huberman. Erik is probably one of the nicest guys out there, but when I asked him why he was such a strong advocate for our brand and what we could do to reward him, he simply said, "You have done such a great job with me, and I think you can help the others in my network."

It was that simple. He felt that we were doing good work for him, and he wanted to tell other people that he thought we could do good work for them, too.

As soon as the words left his mouth, I could almost physically see this trust form around us. This guy was out there helping people—helping others in his network by connecting them to a company that could help and helping our company by being an advocate for us—just because he wanted to be helpful.

To be clear, there are more ways to be a brand advocate than sending introductions someone's way. In fact, it commonly takes the form of content distribution. For example, Matt Heinz of Heinz Marketing comes to mind as someone who advocates for the Influence & Co. brand by sharing our company's content, and each time he does, I think of his brand.

It should therefore come as no surprise that brand advocacy is a direct path to the top of someone's mind. Again, though, authenticity is key—to shill for a brand you don't really care about in the hopes that the company's leadership will notice you is shortsighted. You may even end up damaging the credibility of the company, which is the exact opposite of being helpful.

Provide Referrals

Like brand advocacy, referrals are critical for generating trust around your brand, which invites people to establish direct, powerful connections with your company.

In 2015, 30 percent of our clients at Influence & Co. came through partner referrals, making referrals our largest revenue source. This figure is especially staggering when you consider how many of these referrals took the form of a quick phone call or a casual conversation. These are simple gestures that have tremendous impact. I feel such gratitude to our partners for providing these referrals—each one is a key stakeholder in our growth and success.

Make it a habit that anytime you find out what someone's needs are, you write them down. Someone could be looking for a hire, website designer, way into Google, and so forth. Jot it down. David

Ehrenberg, CEO of Early Growth Financial Services, has driven his company's skyrocketing growth simply by setting goals for referrals to people in its partner network. I know him personally, and he's a naturally helpful person; it makes sense that he feels so strongly about making the right connections for his partner network. (It's almost like a *Field of Dreams* mentality; if you help, opportunities will come.)

Because referrals are such a crucial part of your helpfulness practice, you need a system or even goals (like David has in place) to ensure that you are consistently providing (and collecting) them. Developing a protocol in which you offer a partner referral at certain stages in every strategic relationship can be tremendously helpful, but you have to stay on top of which dots you're connecting. Sometimes keeping track of these relationships is as simple as updating a spreadsheet, but often it requires software such as Contactually or SalesforceIQ to offer more highly targeted help.[4]

Volunteer Your Personal Time

Time is our most valuable asset, so we've got to be efficient with it. But sometimes, all it takes is just a few minutes. Whoever you are and whatever position you hold, you can almost always spare a few minutes now and again.

For example, earlier this year, my cofounder, Kelsey, and I were at an event for an award we had been nominated as finalists for: EY Entrepreneur of the Year. We were busy networking and getting to know the other leaders, but I noticed that the person next to me seemed to be looking for something. When I asked, he said he was looking for a bottle opener.

Without thinking, I got up, quickly walked to a table where I'd seen a bottle opener, and brought it back to him. It wasn't a huge time commitment on my part, but I was able to offer a few minutes of my time to help him. (It turns out he was one of the judges for the event.)

Personal time is both precious and scarce, and we often use it as an excuse to say no. But when you devote a chunk of your personal time to helping others, the gesture is meaningful and memorable.

Every few weeks, I try to do a guest webinar for anyone in my network who is interested. I could easily delegate this responsibility to a team member, but (a) I enjoy doing it and (b) I want my contacts to know that helping them out will always be one of my personal priorities.

Be generous with your time and don't limit your helpfulness to the realm of the professional. Think about the gratitude you feel toward the friend who always helps you move houses or the friend you can call no matter how much time has passed and you still pick up right where you left off. You know the kind of friend I'm talking about: the kind who really sticks with you, whom you can always count on. You're probably already picturing these friends or thinking of the last time they really went out of their way for you. Now what if you applied that same idea to your relationship with a business partner? How would acts of kindness and generosity humanize your professional relationship?

Recognize People

In the early days of Influence & Co., I went out and bought a knockoff pro wrestling championship belt. At our next meeting, Kelsey and I awarded the belt to a team member who had been doing a particularly great job. She was that week's champion, we explained; the next week, it would be up to her to crown a new champion from among her teammates.

As we've grown and spread our team across various cities, awarding the championship belt has gotten a little harder to do. Instead, everyone submits weekly reports on how they're doing, both personally and professionally: what's going well for them, what's frustrating them, what they are excited about. At the end, we ask them to give shout-outs to anyone and everyone who went out of their way to help them—people who did particularly great work, went above and beyond, and helped others. These people's names are passed up to direct supports and our leadership team so everyone is recognized for the awesome work they do.

This sort of recognition works outside your own team, too. When I have a good experience with someone from another company, I'll typically e-mail that person's boss a quick note about my experience. Good work should be recognized; it also feels good to show appreciation. And you never know—people can rise through the ranks pretty quickly, and some day, the person you were advocating for could be in a position to send opportunity your way.

It seems as if every time I fly Southwest Airlines, I end up calling yet another manager to sing the praises of yet another wonderful member of Southwest's ground staff. Not only does this reward the individual whose hard work made my life easier, it strengthens the connection that I have with the brand—the brand that saved my butt earlier this year when I showed up at the wrong airport (who does that?) and needed last-minute exceptions so I could get to my speaking engagement on time.

Sure, Southwest has good customer service. But it had also identified me as someone who'd worked well with its staff, advocated for the airline among other conference speakers I knew, and so on, and it did everything it could to help me when I'd made a complete idiot of myself. Southwest was there for me in my time of need because we had built a relationship together.

Give Gifts

To receive a gift is to experience one of life's simple pleasures. I experienced this pleasure when John Ruhlin, one of the nation's gifting experts and author of *Giftology*, sent me a thank-you gift: a set of high-end personalized Cutco knives. The knives themselves are beautiful, but John's real expertise shines through in the delivery.

Rather than receiving the entire set at once, a couple of personalized knives come every month, thus regularly reminding my wife and me that he exists and is a great guy. Now, I'm not saying that John is innovative simply because he sends personalized knives. What he's done is practice that personalized gifting with a top-of-mind mindset. Giving gifts isn't new, but doing it in a way that reminds both my wife and me each month that he exists has brought a lot of opportunity his way.

(My wife told me once that of anyone who might invite me on a last-minute trip to Las Vegas, John Ruhlin is one of maybe three guys she'd have no problem with. She would be totally cool if I came home and told her, "John just invited me to Vegas with him, but I've got to leave right now." She's never even met him. That's right—John's built this kind of trust with my wife, and they've never met.)

Giving someone a gift is a nice way to establish a personal connection. There are, however, some obvious caveats. When your gifts are expensive or ostentatious, you're flirting with bribery. To say nothing of bribery's legal and ethical implications, I advise you against it mainly because it's ineffective and prevents real trust from forming.

If you want to secure and maintain a position at the top of someone's mind, give gifts that are deeply meaningful to that person and come with no strings attached. You can accomplish more in the long run with a thoughtful or unique gift than you would with a briefcase full of unmarked bills. As my wife would say, "Sometimes it's about the small things."

Take, for example, a senior editor at a major online publication my company works with. We'd been working together for a while, and we knew she had just had a baby. Rather than sending her some big, elaborate gift we thought would make us look nice to give, we specifically went to her registry and ordered a number of small items. We paired the items with personalized notes, coincidentally enough about how important the small things in life are and how excited we were for her.

She later told me that we were the only people in her professional life who took the time to find her registry and give her gifts that she had indicated would be valuable.

Like the other elements of your helpfulness practice, gift giving is more effective when you do it regularly. Aside from using software to keep track of these relationships, there are plenty of niche subscription services that deliver everything from health food and jewelry to gourmet dog treats. Paying for a subscription that matches a client's unique interests is generous and thoughtful and also saves you time.[5]

Personalize Experiences

At the beginning of this chapter, I mentioned caring about people for who they are, not what they can do for you. Beyond knowing who your audience is, a key aspect of caring about people for who they are is understanding that everyone in your audience is an individual—and each of them wants to feel like you're communicating with only him or her.

My friend Rohit Bhargava, author of *Non-Obvious*, explains in his book the importance of personalization. He mentions that Disney spent a billion dollars on personalized magic wristbands and how attendees just loved them. After attending one of his keynotes where he spoke in more detail about this idea, I took my family to Disney World to see for myself.

I loved everything about it.

My daughter, who was two at the time, was so happy and excited. She said, "Daddy, Mickey knew my name!" She felt special, like the whole experience was personalized just for her and all the characters she loved knew who she was. That's how special you want your audience to feel.

I like to think about it like this: James Bond is probably one of the most iconic characters. Wherever he goes, people know his name. You want your audience to feel that special and important. And if you can up the ante by personalizing their experiences to the extent that Disney World did for my daughter, you've got a nearly unbeatable hand. Hotels and resorts have been using tactics like this for a while because the hospitality business is so heavily reliant on customer satisfaction. There's greater competition in every industry, so customer service and engagement have become even more important.

You don't have to spend a billion dollars to create that feeling, though. It sounds clichéd, but handwritten thank you notes can be very meaningful and go a long way to forming closer relationships with people in a digital world taken over by e-mail.

Let me describe a thank you note from my friend John Ruhlin, the gifting expert I mentioned earlier in this chapter, to show his appreciation for our relationship. He included a thoughtful, handwritten note along with a gift for my wife's thirtieth birthday party. In his note, he expressed his appreciation for her and mentioned how much he values the friendship we share. I remember reading it and feeling blown away that he remembered so many details, let alone took the time to write it down and send it with a gift to my wife.

For context, I only mentioned this party to him in passing—it's not like I told him all the details and confirmed my address for him to send a cool present to her. But he remembered, and he ensured the gift she received was personalized for her.

It'd be one thing if he just sent the gift, but he included a special note that made me feel about as special as my daughter did at Disney World. Right then, his status at the top of mind, as a good person and a valuable relationship, was cemented in my long-term memory.

The more personalized you can make your audience's experiences, the more special and valued you will help them feel. Sending thoughtful notes is one tactic. Remembering one detail about each person you meet is another. Next time you're at a conference or event, make an effort to pay close attention and remember one unique detail about everyone you meet. The detail should be more substantive than hair color, for example, or company name. If you're consciously uncovering what people find valuable, you'll very likely come across unique details about them: their struggles at work, their new baby, a sick pet, a move to a different neighborhood. Write down one of these details after your conversations, enter it into your CRM system, and when you follow up after the event, reference the detail. If Lisa told you her youngest child was sick recently, consider opening your follow-up e-mail with, "Hey, Lisa, hopefully you're back home and your son has gotten over the flu you were worried about when we spoke last."

The response rates for e-mails with personal details are much higher than those for e-mails that, for example, say something like "Hey, Lisa, good to meet you. Have you had a chance to talk with your SVP yet?" By personalizing your communication, you're putting yourself in a better place to break down trust barriers.

However, if it's a fast-paced event and you honestly have no time to write down one detail about the people you meet, there is another practice you can try: remember people's names. When someone introduces himself, repeat his name back to him and try to use it a handful of times naturally in your conversation. Then, no matter how many others you've spoken to, go back to everyone whose name you've committed to memory (or, really, added to your phone's contacts) and say goodbye personally, using their names.

Before you (or they) leave, stop by and say, "Hey, Mary, it was good to meet you! I look forward to chatting soon." Not only are people generally surprised when you remember their names, but you get what I call the *American Idol* advantage. As the last person to approach them, engage them, and personalize communication with them, you will be the freshest in their minds, which can work in your favor.

Turning Practice into Habit

If you implement at least a handful of these strategies, you're on your way to developing a comprehensive helpfulness practice. The challenge is to sustain this practice so that it becomes second nature.

To be helpful is to continually connect the dots between people, resources, and opportunities. It is easier to connect the dots when you can see all the dots in one location, such as a spreadsheet or CRM system. A detailed log of connections, referrals, opportunities, and resources can optimize your helpfulness practice. There are plenty of powerful CRM platforms designed to help you do exactly that.[6]

I've said that even the most thoughtful act of kindness will not generate long-term top-of-mind status if it's a one-off. Thriving relationships take time and energy to develop and maintain—to nurture a relationship, you need to engage the person through multiple touch points regularly. Set up a rule for implementing these touch points on a cyclical basis. For example, I try to help out most of my important contacts at least once every three months and others at least once a year.

If that seems daunting, create a set of rules around how much time you want to spend implementing these strategies. Because I write so many referral e-mails, I give myself a three-minute time limit for drafting each one. That allows me to fire off dozens of referrals without getting overwhelmed or derailed. I also use a tool called Mixmax to help me develop some basic templates that I can customize, schedule e-mails, and track opens, clicks, and downloads, but there are tons of tools out there, from Salesforce and Infusionsoft to HubSpot (which my team uses) and more, which you can find in the Resource Library, that can help you make this process faster and easier, too.

Even if you're not a rigid scheduler or you just hate tracking things on spreadsheets or software, you can simply adopt a rule that when people in your network identify something to you that they would really enjoy or would make their lives easier, consider getting it for them. All it takes is listening, and if you embrace this mindset, I assure you that these small changes can make big differences in your relationships.

It doesn't have to be huge. A rule like this wouldn't last very long if everything you got for key members of your audience was extravagant. Simple is usually enough.

One of my key employees looked at my wallet phone case and said, "Man, I need to get one of those. I hate carrying around both." So I went to Amazon, ordered one just like it, and shipped it to his house. It took me all of 30 seconds and $20, and he was so appreciative.

Cultivating Helpfulness Everywhere

I'll be very honest with you: five years ago, this whole chapter would have seemed a little crazy to me, not to mention a big waste of time. But because of the opportunity I've seen come from this mindset and these practices, I'm a believer—and a happier person in general.

Rules and hacks for can be very useful for automating and streamlining your helpfulness practice. However, to truly make helpfulness second nature, you need to integrate it into every aspect of your life.

It could be doing something to help out your partner, brother, sister, friend, or even finding an organization or initiative with a mission that speaks to you; it might be a nonprofit organization, your child's school, and the like. Either way, the more time, energy, and soul you put into helping others—especially when the only thing you stand to gain is personal satisfaction—the more helpfulness becomes a fundamental part of who you are.

Take a minute to write down three ways you can be more helpful to others using the practices from earlier in this chapter. Consider what you'd like to do and how you make its practice a habit. (I promise, it's addictive in the best way.)

Helpfulness Exercise

Think of three people you are close to—friends, family, coworkers you see every day. What do you know about them? Is one of them feeling more stressed out lately? Maybe another recently had a child and could use an extra hand.

Whatever it is, identify one thing that would be valuable to each of them. What can you do to make their lives easier? Is there anything you can do to connect them to that valuable item or favor? I challenge you to act on that.

I further challenge you to do this once a month. As you'll learn, consistency is critical to becoming top of mind, and it's necessary to help train your brain to identify these opportunities for helpfulness more naturally.

4

BEING TRANSPARENT
AND LIKABLE

Social media has radically transformed interpersonal relationships. Never in human history have we had such immediate access to the intimate details of one another's lives.

We can fulfill our nosiest impulses with just a few clicks. In fact, we're so accustomed to life in this state of perpetual exposure that we get suspicious of people who choose to remain private. Think about how rare and strange it is to meet someone without a Facebook account. What's that guy trying to hide, anyway?

This suspicion is even more heightened when it comes to business and political leadership—and certainly more justified. Growing up hearing about Enron, Madoff, and WikiLeaks, our generation has come to associate a lack of transparency with devastating corruption. We've learned to see evil in the opaque.

For all these reasons, nearly every business leader—even the most corrupt—pays lip service to corporate transparency. Thankfully, amid all the hypocrisy and double-talk, there are leaders who take the concept to heart in inspiring ways. Pat Flynn is one of them.

Pat is the entrepreneur behind Smart Passive Income, a website dedicated to teaching people how to launch and run profitable online businesses. Given the common knowledge that many of the people selling products and promising to help you make a ton of money over the Internet are probably con artists, Pat must overcome massive trust barriers to succeed. And by being transparent, this is exactly what he's done.

Every month, Pat posts his monthly income statements on his website. You can see exactly what he's made (or lost) from his own online revenue streams, which is a powerful way to demonstrate the effectiveness of his business methodology. But Pat shares more than just numbers; he also writes about his challenges, failures, and successes as both a businessperson and a father. In the eyes of his followers, Pat's honesty makes him human. (I know Pat personally, and he's also probably one of the happiest people you'll meet.) His audience knows he has nothing to hide, and they reward him with their trust.

In her TED Talk on the power of vulnerability, researcher-storyteller Brené Brown explains, "In order for connection to happen, we have to allow ourselves to be seen—really seen."[1]

What she's saying makes complete sense. We have to be ourselves, and we have to give others a chance to see who we are.

If your business has solid products and great services that are as valuable as they are ethical, you've got nothing to worry about. It's only when you're trying to hide something that transparency poses a threat.

When you're transparent about what you do and why you do it, then there's no worry about something going negatively. Your mind is free of worrying about someone seeing who you are. And that freedom is one of the best feelings in life.

I think we've all seen this at play, especially in our personal lives. For me, I know when I try to keep something from my wife, she'll find out sooner or later. And that whole time between me deciding to keep something under wraps and her learning what it was is filled with anxiety. When I'm honest and transparent about why I did what I did (even if it's a screwup) and what's going on, I feel a sense of freedom.

The tricky thing about transparency is that as much as it benefits you, it can also hurt relationships when it goes untempered by common sense. Let's say my mother-in-law visits and makes a meat loaf using a recipe that's been in the family for generations. This meal looks and smells great, but when I take a bite, the texture is like shoe leather.

In what world would my telling her that benefit either of us? If I said, "Look, Donna, I've got to be transparent with you: this meat loaf is awful," I would only hurt our relationship (and possibly wind up sleeping in my car after my wife heard about it). (Full disclosure: My mother-in-law's meat loaf is perfectly fine.)

Aside from being rude, a statement like that is wrong for a couple of reasons: it was unsolicited, and it wasn't delivered in a constructive way. Now, I understand that sometimes transparency can draw attention to unflattering truths, but that doesn't give you license to broadcast just anything to everyone and their mother (literally, in this case).

Transparency isn't an all-or-nothing arrangement. Of course I try not to beat around the bush, and I strive to be as transparent as I can—but that doesn't mean I'm 100 percent transparent every day about all parts of my life. Your rule of thumb should be to ask yourself, "Is this helpful?" Does it benefit your audience to know this? Does it add to the truth of your relationship with this audience?

In this chapter, we'll discuss what it means to practice authentic transparency and how cultivating a sense of self that is both honest and likable can place you top of mind and lead to exceptional growth.

The Relationship Between Transparency and Trust

Edelman, a global PR and communications firm, releases results of studies on consumer trust in businesses. In one study, 83 percent of U.S. customers indicated that the number one determinant of a company's trustworthiness is whether it has transparent, honest business practices in place.[2] And this goes beyond straightforward service agreements and fair product return policies—consumers demand internal fairness, too.

Remember the uproar in 2015 after the *New York Times* ran an exposé on the "bruising" working conditions at Amazon?[3] Not only were people horrified to read about Amazon employees allegedly weeping at their desks, the public also felt deceived; we had assumed that one of the most innovative tech firms in the world treated its staff more like Google does than Walmart. To hear anything that suggested otherwise dealt a blow to Jeff Bezos's credibility (at least until he and other "Amazonians" shared content that painted a different picture entirely).[4]

The second most important factor in developing consumer trust is the quality of the products and services that a company provides. Again, transparency plays a vital role.

Consider, for instance, the story of Mast Brothers chocolate. The Masts are bearded Brooklyn-based chocolatiers who tout themselves as pioneers of the bean-to-bar artisanal chocolate movement. But in late 2015, allegations emerged that throughout the early days of the company, Mast was making bars by melting down commercially produced French chocolate and repackaging it as "original"—a pretty big detour on the path from bean to bar.

Quartz published a piece called "How the Mast Brothers Fooled the World into Paying $10 a Bar for Crappy Hipster Chocolate."[5] *Vanity Fair*, CNBC, and the *Guardian* covered the controversy, and Mast sales plunged. Regardless of what's being misrepresented, whether it's your process, your products, or anything else, the risks are always greater than any perceived reward. Transparency and authenticity matter.

Finally, the third and most important factor in determining a company's trustworthiness is how it communicates with the outside world. Even if you're running a great business, failing to engage your customer base in an ongoing conversation is the equivalent of withholding information.

To generate trust, you need to create a relationship; for that to happen, you need to open up lines of communication that are honest, meaningful, and authentic. Remember, relationships emerge between people, not between people and a faceless brand. Therefore, it's vital that you provide an opportunity for your customer base—as well as the rest of your network—to connect directly to the people who make up your brand.

And it starts with you.

The Evolution of Personal Branding to Thought Leadership and Company Branding

Debating whether to invest significant time and resources into your brand isn't really an option anymore. Simply put, it is nearly impossible to survive—much less succeed—in this You Marketing landscape without a thriving personal brand. The most obvious motivation is for your own self-investment. Imagine a 401(k) plan investment: To live your dream, you have to consistently invest over time. But it's valuable for more than what it can do for you alone. The evolution of personal branding has made it a necessary strategy for companies, too.

Before we go any further, I want to clarify some terms. In this chapter, I'll be exploring the evolution from personal branding to thought leadership and why the intersection between personal branding and company branding led to this change.

Personal branding has been around forever. Experts such as William Arruda, Dorie Clark, and Dan Schawbel, among others, have been preaching about its importance for years. However, it wasn't until recently that the term *thought leadership* grew into such a buzzword. That change was necessary because there needed to be a different term that connected the dots between personal branding and its benefits to a company as a whole.

"Personal" is a word that implies one individual and screams ego stroking—not the beginnings of a solid company strategy. But in reality, if personal branding is done right and leveraged across your company, it can be one of your most important company branding tactics.

Being strategic about your investments in key employees' personal branding can pay off.

Encouraging your key employees to share unique experience and expertise with your target audience through digital content, social media, speaking engagements, and the like, can clearly have a big benefit for the company, and it's not just about the individual anymore. If the strategy is put together well, it can benefit how your company shows up for search when people are looking for areas around your service, help you connect with potential recruits, or even train new employees with the content you are creating from these key players.

That said, designating one or two leaders to represent the company's brand doesn't mean that the rest of the team fades into the background and goes unnoticed. The actions of all employees reflect on the business, so the stronger their various personal brands, the better. A team with multiple thought leaders quickly generates a reputation for being an innovative powerhouse.

Further, it doesn't mean that only your senior-level executives can be thought leaders. If you've built a good company, you've got a lot of really smart people working together, and anyone can (and should) practice and build thought leadership within a company.

Honestly, of all the assets your company possesses, the knowledge of your employees is the biggest and most important differentiating factor. Those insights are unique to those individuals, and they work for your company—building thought leadership around that expertise sets you apart from competitors and offers your audience more opportunities to connect with your brand.

When we started Influence & Co., we worked almost exclusively with execs and entrepreneurs. Since then, the fire has caught on, and employees throughout companies are eager to communicate their expertise, too. From engineers who can explain the newest technological advances to the sales team that knows exactly what content its leads are asking for, the thought leadership trend has extended beyond the C-suite. Subject matter experts are now building their authority because they know exactly how it can help their teams accomplish goals while also amplifying their companies' brands.

Let's assume that of all the smart people in your organization, you (and your brand) are among those selected to represent the company. As a public representative of the business, you have a serious responsibility to make the language, messaging, and marketing goals of the company your own. But you also have a responsibility to your own voice—because if you're not authentic, you're a thinly veiled marketing gimmick. And gimmicks have a hard time forming lasting relationships.

How do you maintain individual personality while representing your company? How can a personal brand be both compelling and on-message to make sure it represents the business well?

Here are a few guiding principles for achieving just that:

Limit Obnoxious Self-Promotion

Yes, the concept of personal branding may sound inherently narcissistic, and the narcissism endemic to social media only makes things worse. But don't let that fool you.

Remember, your goal is to build meaningful relationships. For that to happen, you need to open up to your audience, sharing your insight and experience in a way that is honest, transparent, and human. Only when you present yourself as a real person—flaws, failures, and all—will you build a real bond with your audience.

In a webinar for *Inc.* columnists, Jeff Haden was asked how he achieves such massive engagement numbers on his content. He said that he puts himself in his audience's shoes, does his best to honestly think about what would engage them the most, and then marries his own knowledge and experiences with that information. Notice that at no point in this process does Jeff strategize on how to promote himself or put his needs above his audience's. That's the key.

As I mentioned earlier in this book, I've absolutely ridden the narcissistic roller coaster, and all it ever did was weaken my relationships and make me feel a little empty inside. I learned my lesson: I worked first on controlling my self-promotion (or my own bragging and exaggerating) among my friends, and soon that self-control became habitual and spilled into my professional life.

Is it great to hear other people celebrate my success or the success of my company? Of course. And when you avoid blatant self-promotion and focus instead on the needs of your audience, you'll build a loyal enough following that when something worth celebrating happens, your advocates will be singing your praises.

Always Deliver Value

Authenticity is the foundation of your relationship with your audience. But for the relationship to flourish, it's not enough to simply be authentic; you also have to deliver tangible value. You have to make life better or easier for your audience, not just tell honest stories about yourself.

So how do you know what's really valuable? It's simple: ask. You are the best researcher you will ever have. Reach out to your audience and ask what would be valuable to them. Pay attention to what topics and formats of communication they've engaged with in the past; is your audience interested in revisiting those ideas? You won't know until you ask.

I used to make the classic mistake my wife points out sometimes: I acted before listening or thinking all the way through something first. I used to write about what I thought was interesting or what I thought would be valuable to my audience. Now I ask. Over time, you'll start to notice patterns of what your most important audiences find valuable, and that will make the process even easier.

The idea with thought leadership is that by sharing your knowledge and expertise, you're adding value to your audience's lives through education. This education could come in the form of an insightful conversation in a bar with one person or in a crowd of thousands listening to a keynote speaker share her expertise.

It could be delivered through a comprehensive white paper exploring industry trends and best practices, a simple blog post celebrating the unique contributions of a fellow leader, or an article about work-life balance. Whatever the format or topic, everything you communicate should enhance the lives of your audience in some way.

Does it have to be a topic in which you have expertise? Not quite. When my daughter was born, I struggled with taking paternity leave for the first time, even though we had just adopted a new paternity policy and I knew I needed to lead by example. But the most I'd ever taken off work was five days, and now I was expected to take off six weeks? I didn't think I'd make it. (I didn't. I made it for three and a half weeks.)

When I got back, though, many friends, partners, and clients asked how it was. Honestly, I enjoyed it, and when I shared that with other workaholics, they were interested. Some recommended I write an article about it. The first article I published when I returned to work was about my leave, and it did really well.

Am I an expert on paternity leave? Absolutely not. Am I an expert in anything related to time off? Nope. What qualified me to write this article was my real-world experience struggling with this decision that ended up being incredibly valuable for me—and of course my audience's request. While I mostly share content about topics such as leadership, sales, content marketing, and PR, I understand that it's OK to communicate insights outside of those areas of expertise if my audience finds it valuable and easier to connect with me on a human level, too.

Take a moment to think about the experiences you've had that could enhance the lives of your target audience. Write down your topic and start keeping a bank of these ideas. When you get a little more time on the side, start writing and see where it takes you.

Tackle Real Issues and Be Smart About It

Although there is certainly value in making your audience smile, one can take only so many memes. Pumping your audience full of fluff is a surefire way to lose their attention; if you don't say anything meaningful, people will stop listening. Show your audience that you respect their intelligence, and make a habit of tackling real issues. Don't shy away from controversy, and don't be afraid to be honest. That said, be strategic: if you're not well educated about a controversial topic, don't weigh in. There is no point in simply adding to the noise.

And if you ever find yourself at the center of controversy, the way Apple did with the FBI in 2016, you'd do well to surround yourself with content that addresses it head-on. I use Apple as an example because the open letter that CEO Tim Cook published[6] did a fantastic job of tackling real issues of personal privacy and security—and it was a smart approach.

The controversy began when the FBI asked Apple to unlock the iPhone of the San Bernardino terrorist. Apple refused because of the security risk it posed to users of Apple products. When headlines accused Apple of siding with the terrorist, Apple took a strong public stance—which was risky.

On behalf of the company, Tim Cook wrote:

> We have great respect for the professionals at the FBI, and we believe their intentions are good. Up to this point, we have done everything that is both within our power and within the law to help them. But now the U.S. government has asked us for something we simply do not have, and something we consider too dangerous to create. They have asked us to build a backdoor to the iPhone.

He continued by explaining explicitly why Apple refused to comply, ending with the following statement:

> We are challenging the FBI's demands with the deepest respect for American democracy and a love of our country. We believe it would be in the best interest of everyone to step back and consider the implications. While we believe the FBI's intentions are good, it would be wrong for the government to force us to build a backdoor into our products. And ultimately, we fear that this demand would undermine the very freedoms and liberty our government is meant to protect.

From a business perspective, that willingness to prioritize its consumers and stand by their security offered a competitive advantage: this is a company that's going to bat for you and your privacy, and you can trust it completely. That's huge.

Other controversial topics require thoughtful, constructive conversation, and when industry experts contribute to those conversations in a respectful way, they can position themselves as trusted leaders in those spaces.

Take my brother, for example. He's a defense attorney who makes it a priority to educate his audience on changes to legislation that are complicated or controversial. His firm's blog has a "need to know" section that explains these changes in a way that's easy to digest, so the average person can understand how the new laws might affect him or her.

Is he a content marketing expert? No, not by a long shot. But he has created a trusted resource for many to learn about otherwise complex and controversial issues that may affect their lives. By tackling real issues, and doing so strategically, he's been able to grow his law firm substantially.

Commit to Consistency

There's nothing quite so disappointing as reading a mind-blowing article, only to discover that the author never published another post. There you are, looking for what else this amazing author has written—but when you search, you find nothing. That was it. That article is all there is, and you've already read it. What do you do now?

If that example doesn't resonate with you, consider how things would be different if J. K. Rowling called it a day after the first Harry Potter book. Or if she wrote the first book, took a couple years off, wrote another one or two in the series, and went on hiatus again for six years. The lack of consistency would have devastated a generation of fans.

Consistency is comforting. It lets your audience know what to expect and when they can expect it, which keeps them engaged and gives you more opportunities to connect with them over time—and earn top-of-mind space.

As we'll talk about in the next chapter, branding is much like working out. The lasting health benefits of an annual day of exercise, no matter how strenuous, are minimal. To effectively build and leverage your brand to grow your company, you've got to keep at it.

Be Prepared for Content Triggers

As I discussed earlier, content triggers are conversations that inspire aha moments about your industry or your clients' needs. Triggers often present themselves in fleeting moments, so be alert and diligent. Once you've been triggered for content, keep track of your content topics, ideas, and commentary. My team and I use our proprietary software to create knowledge banks that store and organize those ideas, and we use the same process for clients.[7]

A knowledge bank is a centralized location for storing and cataloging your team's ideas, insights, content triggers, and experiences so they can be accessed easily when you're creating content. Banking that knowledge and keeping all your triggers and relevant ideas in one place makes it easier and faster to create authentic, engaging content in the future.

How do you fill up your knowledge bank? Send a quick message to anyone on your team who's in regular contact with members of your most valued audiences. These could be your client service team leaders, salespeople, support specialists—anyone who's hearing firsthand from audiences. Remind them that as team members on the front lines, they're your best researchers, and you'll reward them for any information they can share that helps you better understand your audience. Make it a contest to see who can add the most information to your knowledge bank, and award that quarter's winner with a prize or bonus or something else the person finds valuable.

Whether it's recurring questions from clients, common pain points and objections your sales team is facing, or something else entirely, these are valuable triggers for content—and they're perfect for filling up the bank.

Distribute Through the Right Channels, Not Just the Ones You Think Are Cool

It's critical to maintain a vibrant presence on your company's owned media (your company blog, social media profiles, e-mail marketing, etc.), but this is only one piece of the puzzle (or inbound funnel, if you will). Your audience reads and follows other types of media—media that you don't control. To get your ideas delivered to them, sometimes you've got to earn that media, and that often takes the form of guest-contributed content, PR, social media, and so forth.

It's important to realize that distribution can take many forms. I categorize it as any tactic used to reach an audience you're trying to influence. Maybe it's a social media push with a little spend behind it, or maybe it's a paid influencer marketing strategy designed to get more eyes on your content while it has a giant trust stamp from your favorite influencer.

Those are great tactics, and they can be very effective. But I always recommend starting with earned distribution first. If you earn your own influence first, that puts you in a position to land valuable tactics for free—influencer partnerships, for example. This is much more powerful than running out of the gate throwing money at all your options.

A lot of companies begin sponsoring conferences or paying for expensive ads on different sites and never see the ROI because they're not even sure if they're going after the right audiences. My team has focused on earned opportunities for speaking or content contribution, and in four years, we didn't spend a dime on sponsorships.

We accomplished this by building our own influence first and becoming the source of information and engagement that people wanted to host at their events. We learned what events work for us and what events don't, which puts us in a much better position to put spend behind the right events in the future.

The same goes for our content. We've earned our bylines in virtually every publication in our industry, and we know what performs well—and what doesn't. Now we're able to execute paid amplification strategies to distribute that content to a larger audience, and we're even able to offer content for other contributors and influencers to source in their articles, keynotes, social media, and more. As a result, we're in a position to guide the conversation about our brand and help shape much of the content out there in our industry.

I find myself referring to this state—a state in which so much of the content in our industry is coming from us or from other influencers who've used our content as a source for information—as a content utopia. Imagine yourself in this utopia: every piece of content you want about your brand and your company is out there, coming either directly from you or from someone else your audience trusts. It's published in a variety of outlets and promoted through platforms that enable you to reach your audience consistently. And because it's published and in front of the right people, your audience and peers are talking about you in the exact way you want to be talked about.

This utopia used to be nearly nonexistent, and honestly, it still takes work to achieve. But now, with the right strategy, a process for documenting and acting on content triggers, and a plan for execution, you can make it happen. My team and I have seen it happen time and time again. A company can go from no online presence to industry domination with the right content that's distributed to the right people and places.

Remember not to fall into the cool distribution trap. Don't waste your time targeting publications or events that you think are cool. It's not about you—it's about your audience. Where are they? What are they reading? How can you get in front of them?

Don't let yourself become distracted by big names just because they sound impressive or because your competitors are over there.

I won't lie: this is difficult. But earning a byline in a publication such as *Forbes*, for example, isn't meant to be refrigerator material for your mom.

Above all, understand that to rely solely on publications for distribution is to leave opportunity on the floor. Publications—even the most reputable, highest-level marquee names—are vehicles to build authority and tap into an existing audience. It's your responsibility to maximize that reach and further distribute and promote your content through methods such as paid advertisements, social posts, influencer marketing relationships, and so on.

The Importance of Likability

One of my favorite basketball players is Stephen Curry. He's great at what he does, and he seems like a genuinely good guy. So whenever I'm talking with someone about basketball, guess who's the first person to come to mind?

Naturally, you're more inclined to advocate for people and brands that you like over those you feel neutral or even negatively about. That's part of the power of being likable. It sounds simple, but it's one of the most powerful top-of-mind tools.

Still, it's impossible to be likable and flawless all the time. Try as you might, you can't avoid the occasional bad day, and you can't guarantee that every interaction you have with your audience will be perfect. Sometimes they just won't have the best experience with you, and without likability and a record of overall competence, you risk negative brand advocacy.

When you're in this position, you can hope for one of two things: your audience is full of supernice people who would never speak negatively about a brand, or your audience trusts and likes you enough to understand that mistakes happen.

Nobody is perfect, not even brands with entire teams devoted to service and communication. When we started as a company, did we have the best service? No, we did not. We were (and still are) learning and growing every day. It's taken a lot for us to become the company we are today, and fortunately, clients liked and believed in us enough to give us helpful feedback and support us.

It bought us some time in those early phases and gave us insights into how to improve so that now, years later, our service is much better. You aren't going to master customer relationships 100 percent of the time, but if people like you and your brand, they'll give you a chance to recover so that the occasional mistake won't derail your company.

It's also worth considering that in the market, there's almost always a cheaper option. And if you're the cheapest option now, chances are that you might not be in the future. But providing good service and having a likable brand can help keep your clients from shopping around for a different company. For example, I find the employees of Southwest very likable, and that translates to finding the brand itself likable. Are they always the cheapest option? No. Do they ever make mistakes? Sure, who doesn't? But because of their likability, I regularly fly Southwest. So, ultimately, their likability gives them a competitive advantage.

Cultivating Likability

One aspect often missing from conversations about transparency is the impact that likability has on personal and company branding efforts. The two concepts are interrelated: Likability without transparency is shallow, and transparency without likability can be off-putting. And yet if you try too hard to get people to like you, you risk coming off as disingenuous, which will kill any attempt you make to connect with people.

So what does it mean to be authentically likable?

To answer this question, it's helpful to stop thinking of likability as a trait that you either have or don't have. Just as there are various types of intelligence, likability manifests in different forms.

The most obvious form is what I call "Paul Rudd" likability. Because who doesn't love Paul Rudd? He's a great actor who also seems to be a genuinely funny, charming, and self-effacing person. Whenever he's in a movie, I drag my wife to the theater in the hopes that Paul may be in the audience and might want to hang out afterward. (Paul, if you're reading this, please call me.) Paul Rudd likability is easygoing and natural, though that's right about where it stops.

Then you've got my high school English teacher, Matt Clark. As a student, I didn't particularly like Mr. Clark, mainly because he made us read a classic work of literature every week. Seriously, we had a handful of days to make it through all 600-plus pages of *Moby-Dick*.

Today, though, I consider Mr. Clark to be one of the greatest teachers I've ever had. Did I find him relatable? Nope. (I don't think I ever saw him outside of class in one of those surreal moments when you see that your teacher is a real person with interests and errands to run when he's not assigning you more homework.) But is he still likable? Yes. Thanks to him, I developed a pretty good understanding of Western literature, which I believe makes me a more well-rounded person. Matt Clark represents a very nuanced form of likability; it emerges not from the ability to pal around with you but from the great respect you develop for someone who pushes you to become your best self.

Then there's Oprah.

Oprah is one of the most powerful and influential people in the world, and she didn't get that way by being either completely fun (like Paul Rudd) or completely challenging (like Mr. Clark). Her show gives you a good idea of what I mean. Its focus wasn't just "We're here to have a blast!" Sure, she made it fun and enjoyable, but she didn't shy away from difficult, sometimes even controversial, issues either. She shined a light on topics that could make you uncomfortable and force you to think about things differently, but she did it in such an approachable way that you could tell she cared even as she challenged you.

Think about which one of these profiles resonates with you. Are you a happy person who prefers to have fun and get along without confrontation? You're a Paul Rudd. If you couldn't care less about whether people want to be your buddy but instead find joy in pushing others to be better versions of themselves, you're a Mr. Clark. Or do you find yourself striking a balance between the two, prioritizing neither the "fun friend" nor the "tough teacher" but striving to represent both? If so, you might be an Oprah.

As a concept, likability is expansive, complex, and fluid, and it manifests itself in infinitely diverse ways. Sometimes it boils down to personality, but being cognizant of a few key ways to be likable can help you see where you fall on the spectrum and find a path to improving, should you discover you're too far on one side.

These three figures represent a narrow sample; still, I find them a useful launch point for contemplating authentic likability. Personally, I shoot for the friendly-challenger balance of likability that Oprah personifies—it's important for people to respect you because you bring out the best in them, but it would be ideal if they also enjoy being around you.

Developing a Practice of Authentic Likability

Like helpfulness, authentic likability is a practice. It can't be forced, but it can be developed through everyday thoughts and actions. In Chapter 2, I mentioned an article by Jeff Haden that made me realize I could be doing more to develop my likability. This was a powerful reminder to be more aware of how I present myself. It's tough to look at yourself honestly and realize that you're falling short in so many areas.

I put this list in its entirety here for you to explore and walk through the same process I did.

According to Jeff, likable people always:

1. Shift the spotlight to others.
   This is something I do, but not with enough frequency. I need to improve.

2. Listen a lot more than they talk.
   I'm a talker, but I'm not a bad listener. I'll never nail this one, but I can always do better.

3. Don't practice selective hearing.
   I understand it can be devastating, and I work hard to listen well. Not only will you make worse decisions if you lack all the necessary information, but you'll hurt your relationships, too. (My wife would say I'm a work in progress on this one.)

4. Are thoughtful simply because they want to be.
   I agree and believe that I make a genuine effort here.

5. Put their stuff away (meaning they don't check their phones, laptops, or watches during conversations).
   I never used to put all my things away. I always had at least my phone out in meetings. I'd say I put things away closer to 90 percent of the time now, so I can focus on the conversation, which leaves me about 10 percent's worth of room to keep improving.

6. Give before they receive—and sometimes they *never* receive.
   I truly believe in this one and do my best to live my life this way— which is why it's a central theme of this book.

7. Don't act self-important . . .
   Failing grade here. As my influence has grown, so has my ego. I've worked very hard to turn this around, but it's a work in progress.

8. Because they realize other people are more important.
I feel confident about this.

9. Choose their words.
This wasn't something I used to do, but it's now a habit I practice regularly. Slight adjustments in wording or tone can completely change a conversation.

10. Don't discuss the failings of others . . .
As a kid, I was a brat about this. I thought it made me feel better, but I've learned that celebrating others' failure is never acceptable (even if it is a competitor). You should focus on succeeding yourself; focusing on others' mistakes distracts you from your own work.

11. But readily admit their failings
I'm a straightforward person and can typically admit my failings (at least to myself). I could probably be more transparent about this.

Well, you've seen the process I took going through this article. I strongly encourage you to do it yourself and feel free to pull from other lists. If being likable is something you want to accomplish, you've got to work to become self-aware enough to achieve that.

It's easy to be a friendly, accessible person when you're in a good mood and surrounded by people with whom you already have strong relationships. The challenge is to remain authentically likable when you're frustrated, tired, and trying to engage people you don't know.

Authentic likability is a practice that requires commitment and humility. And there's far more to it than simply following a checklist. If you demand that people like you—in other words, if you feel entitled to their good graces—you'll come across as shallow and conceited, no matter how meticulously you follow Jeff's advice.

The key is to act with a sense of true intention. Be deliberate, open, and humble. To ensure that your practice is authentic, try making your own list. Think of the people you find charming, accessible, and inspiring, and list their most likable attributes. Experiment with putting these qualities into practice yourself and seek out others who embody them as well. Developing relationships with likable people will help you hone your practice.

Remember, likability is something that confounds even (or perhaps especially) the most successful people—so be patient with yourself.

Being Your Likable Self in Branding

When you think of likability, it may be easy to limit your thoughts to those you meet in person in your day-to-day life. You either like people or you don't, and when you're with them in person that likability (or lack thereof) is obvious. But the truth is, all of these principles of likability are just as relevant to the world of branding and online content as they are to your personal interactions.

For example, whether you're writing a status update or a book, your personality comes across. When you communicate from a place of self-importance, you will just as quickly alienate your audience as if you were physically in the same room. And thanks to the Internet's affinity for sharing and shaming pretentious content—from tweets and memes to cringeworthy videos and everything in between—you'll be alienating a much larger group of people.

Consider this: any piece of your content could potentially form someone's first impression of you. I know that all of us would like to think that we could look past a bad first impression, but the truth is, it's really hard to do. It takes time and a lot of mental energy and effort to reconsider how we think of someone, and even then, if we do commit to putting in the work, it's hard to reverse a bad impression.

Researchers from the University of Chicago explored that idea to see what it takes to shift perceptions, otherwise called the tipping point of moral change. Their findings showed that "people require more evidence to perceive improvement than decline; it is apparently easier to become a sinner than a saint."[8]

If you publish content that doesn't reflect who you are or is not high quality, two things can happen: you either give a bad first impression or you contribute to what little evidence people need to perceive decline.

So present yourself as authentically and honestly as possible as consistently as you can. Any update or article or speech could very well be someone's first encounter with you (online or offline). It takes more time and effort to undo a bad impression than to make a good one in the first place.

Communicate as if you *were* in the same room as your audience. Present yourself accessibly and personably. In everything you create, give your audience the opportunity to connect.

When they do connect by commenting or reaching out over social media, don't ignore them (unless they're trolls). Social media gives you a platform to have substantive, ongoing conversations with your audience, which makes it a vital part of forging the meaningful relationships that will keep you top of mind throughout your network.

Ultimately, the bottom line is this: be yourself but challenge yourself. Everyone is capable of being authentically transparent and likeable. All it takes is energy, focus, and intention.

Likability Exercise

Set aside time this week for some self-reflection. Search the Internet, think about your friends, family, mentors, partners, and so on, and identify five traits of the people and companies you find most likable. What do these people and companies have in common? What traits do you value? Now (here comes the hard part), be honest with yourself: Do you embody these traits? Are you really doing all you can to put these ideas into practice?

Reach out to someone you respect, someone you know will be honest and direct with you. Ask for this person's help and work with him or her to put together a plan for improvement.

5

REMAINING CONSISTENT AND BOOSTING FAMILIARITY

A TALE OF two executives:

On November 12, 2013, MasterCard CEO Ajay Banga published his debut post as a LinkedIn Influencer. Within hours of being published, *Financial Inclusion by 2020: Our Generation's Equivalent of Putting a Man on the Moon* had generated tens of thousands of views, thousands of shares, and hundreds of LinkedIn comments.[1] Ajay had started a compelling conversation, and people around the world were highly engaged.

Nearly three and a half years later, Mr. Banga has not responded to a single reader comment. Far more frustrating, however, is that after generating so much momentum with this first post, he never wrote a second.

Compare Mr. Banga's output to that of Dharmesh Shah, cofounder of HubSpot. Dharmesh became a LinkedIn Influencer in 2012, and within his first nine months alone, he had already published

30 articles. Each generated an average of 123,000 views—with his most popular one hitting 1.2 million, along with 4,200 comments.

Today more than 620,000 people follow Dharmesh's Influencer profile, a readership twice as large as Ajay Banga's. Dharmesh has shown the same commitment to consistent publishing through Twitter, the HubSpot blog, and his other website, OnStartups.com. Not only have these resources become some of the most trusted, beloved sources of knowledge in online marketing, Dharmesh now is regarded as one of the most influential thought leaders in the business.

Maybe it isn't a big deal that Ajay Banga has only ever published one piece. After all, he's the CEO of one of the world's largest, most powerful multinational corporations; will his lack of consistency on LinkedIn really make a difference to MasterCard's bottom line? Compared with MasterCard, HubSpot is minuscule; therefore, Dharmesh *has* to scramble to make his voice consistently heard in order to survive. Because the stakes are lower for Ajay, he can afford to remain idle.

That's a cynical assessment, and there's certainly some truth to it. However, it's also true that MasterCard's size doesn't guarantee a competitive advantage. The company's success depends on the strength of its relationships with its customers, investors, and partners. To pass up any opportunity to enhance and expand on those relationships *is* a big deal.

If the thought of taking HubSpot and Dharmesh Shah's lead and publishing a consistent stream of content makes you cringe, you're not alone. How many times have you visited a company's blog only to find that it hasn't been updated for the last six months? Or looked up some Fortune 100 CEO on Twitter to discover that her last tweet was in 2012? Clicking through neglected content streams feels a bit like tiptoeing through an old graveyard. It's almost as if you're trespassing in a place you're not supposed to be—not exactly the feeling you want to inspire in your clients.

The concept of thought leadership is one loaded with nuance and complexity. There are no hard-and-fast rules except for one: if you are not consistent, you are not a thought leader.

The Relationship Between Consistency, Memory, and Top-of-Mind Status

I want to revisit a metaphor. In Chapter 2, I compared building trust to making a campfire. But you can't simply start a bright, beautiful fire and then walk off. A fire needs a constant supply of oxygen and fuel to survive, so it's up to you to fan the flames, rearrange the wood, and add new logs as needed. If you turn your back on it for too long, your fire burns out.

The same is true for thought leadership. You could publish the perfect piece of content—one that sparks millions of views, shares, and comments—and you'd skyrocket to top-of-mind status very quickly. But getting to the top doesn't guarantee you'll stay there; thanks to our ever-shrinking attention spans, it's a precarious position to occupy. If you wait too long to publish your next piece, the audience that once hung on your every word will soon forget you.

An industry leader is someone who bridges the gap between her audience's short-term and long-term memory. Short-term memory is seriously short: on average, we have the capacity to simultaneously retain seven pieces of information, but only for about 20 seconds.[2] In light of the staggering amount of information we process on a second-to-second basis, short-term memory is like quicksand.

For short-term memory to enter the long term, a neurological process called consolidation has to occur, during which neurons in the brain rearrange themselves. According to Alison Preston, assistant professor at the University of Texas at Austin Center for Learning and Memory, consolidation doesn't happen instantaneously;

it requires the passage of time. It can take minutes, hours, or even years to develop long-term memories.[3]

Allow me to illustrate this with an embarrassing case study from my own life.

When I was six, my older sister taught me the Cabbage Patch Kids song, and she'd make me perform it anytime her friends were around. (Go ahead, imagine it.)

I'm not exactly sure how long it took for the words to sear themselves into my long-term memory, but by the time I was about seven, I knew every single word by heart. And she and her friends just loved it.

Like a lot of kids, I was a bit of a ham; I knew that they'd laugh and cheer if I performed it, and I took advantage of that. I learned what would be valuable to them, and I did my best to deliver. My sister got married this year, and leading up to it, she and her friends told me how they still remember those moments.

Things really haven't changed all that much. I still know every word of the Cabbage Patch Kids song, which is why every karaoke night ends with me howling, "*There will be laughter in the cabbage patch againnnn!*" And I still do my best to deliver what my audience finds valuable.

Though strange, this demonstrates the vital role that consistency plays in creating long-term memories. When I explained this example to Paul Spiegelman, an expert in company culture, he said, "John, I want to be for my audience what this Cabbage Patch Kids song has been for you. I want to stick with them for life and be so memorable that I pop up in their minds when they think of anything company culture–related."

His goal is one that all leaders should share. You want your brand and your company to be what your audience thinks of when they hear news, information, stories, or anything else related to what you do. That's valuable real estate. Consider the benefits someone like Elon Musk has reaped because people think of him and his companies when they think of business, technology, and innovation. When you are exposed consistently to something over a long period, it becomes familiar and easy to recall. When that something is someone's face, voice, or personality, the familiarity you feel goes a long way toward becoming top of mind. But achieving familiarity is not the same as becoming a thought leader; it's only a first step.

Consistency, Quality, and Credibility

How many of you or your family members talk about the good old days when kids could ride their bikes and play all day without the fear of some creep bothering them (or worse)? You probably hear awful news stories all the time, and this bias that humans have, called the availability heuristic,[4] can make you think that it's more dangerous than ever because it seems like all you ever hear is terrible news.

When the news regularly focuses more on the risks and dangers around us than on all the good things that actually do happen, a kind of shortcut forms in our brains, and that negative information is what we retrieve most easily. That doesn't mean kids are necessarily in more danger today than kids a generation or two ago were. It just means that the last thing you probably heard, read, or saw was negative and scary, and you've heard it pretty frequently, so that's the information you draw on to make a decision or judgment.

Psychologists studied this idea decades ago and realized that people use examples they can immediately recall to help form their opinions (as opposed to collecting and analyzing all the data to make rational and entirely fact-based decisions).

I used the news example because I think we've all experienced hearing more bad news than good in most media, but this idea manifests itself in so many other ways, too.

For example, close your eyes and think of your least favorite band of all time, the one that reaches new depths of awfulness with every song it releases. It's easy to envision the lead singer's smug face as he blurts out those terrible lyrics in that hyperannoying voice, right?

Sorry to evoke such an unpleasant image, but I was only proving a point. The type of familiarity bred by consistency is directly related to the quality of the output. You're quite familiar with your least favorite band in the world, but your familiarity takes the form of loathing.

Consistent quality, in contrast, generates credibility and helps people form positive opinions and judgments.

This time, I'd like for you to think of an actor or actress who consistently delivers unbelievable performances, someone who is an icon in the industry.

Did you picture Meryl Streep (or even someone like Britney Spears in *Crossroads*)?

All joking aside, whether you pictured Meryl Streep or someone else, we should strive to be a little more like those who always deliver outstanding work. Meryl, for example, consistently makes a mark in every movie she's in, and many will probably say that she was great in the last film they saw her in. She's an authentic, talented actress who enhances lives through her work, and her audience can recall her regular and most recent performances as positive ones. The same goes for being an expert in your industry.

All this to say that if you can regularly engage people and add value to their lives—through your speaking engagements, through your personal communications, and, importantly, through your content—you'll develop a familiarity that breaks down trust barriers and puts you top of mind. With this kind of familiarity, you can attract a following, connect to your audience, and, ultimately, become an industry authority.

But this authority, this thought leadership, isn't an end unto itself. It's a way to forge and maintain thriving relationships, which means that you never stop improving the lives of your audience.

That's why your content output is so critical—you need to engage your audience consistently, but there's a physical limit to the number of conferences, networking sessions, and retreats you can attend. You can go to only so many events and meet so many people in any given amount of time.

Content enables you to open up a direct line of communication through which you can engage your audience, and it is by far the most scalable way to do so. With one article, one piece of content online, I can reach a huge audience—people I don't have the time or physical ability to meet with one on one.

Content, in all its forms, is an effective and scalable way to build your authority and enter into a living, breathing conversation with your audience that doesn't end.

As Kelsey says, the old adage "it's not a sprint; it's a marathon" doesn't actually apply to industry authority because there's no real finish line. Rather than thinking of it as a race of any length, Kelsey talks about thought leadership as a fit and healthy lifestyle.[5] Your long-term health requires daily discipline; so, too, does creating that vibrant, ever-evolving conversation with your audience.

Don't be intimidated by the phrase "daily discipline." By setting up process-oriented workflows and creative rituals, you can make consistent content production second nature.

Painless Consistency Through Creative Ritual

The Artist's Way is Julia Cameron's classic guide to channeling your creative potential. In the book, Cameron explains that inspiration is fickle; if you wait for it to strike, you'll create very little in life. Instead, it's exponentially more productive to build creative rituals into your daily routine (such as writing my "morning pages," three pages of stream of consciousness every morning). Daily practice nourishes your inner artist and boosts your creative output.

I mention writing here because, all "content" aside, the act of putting your thoughts down in the form of the written word can be an effective way of training your brain to stay sharp and foster creativity. I've found that writing a few pages in stream-of-consciousness style in the mornings keeps me on my toes on calls and attentive in my interactions with others throughout the day.

I bring this up because "I don't know what to write about" is the second most common excuse I hear from would-be industry leaders who are struggling to begin creating content. The first is a complete and utter lack of time—and neither excuse holds up.

Cameron's emphasis on the power of creative rituals dismantles both of these rationalizations. Not only does routine help you carve out and protect regularly scheduled writing time, it also hones your ability to transform ideas into the written word. The more often you create, the easier—and more enjoyable—the process becomes.

Ultimately, consistency breeds consistency. But don't let devotion to a routine sap the fun out of everything. If your regular writing sessions feel like a chore, take a look at what you're doing from a different perspective. Thought leadership is an opportunity to build compelling dialogue and foster enriching conversations about the most interesting aspects of your industry. This is a real privilege— one that can make life better not only for your audience but for you as well.

Consistency Exercise

The biggest factors in achieving consistency are the tools and processes you put in place to help you. You're only human, and you'll likely forget things or reorganize your priorities, and consistency can fall easily by the wayside. That's why your organization is important here.

You do so many things every day that could be scaled or practiced more consistently—but to do that, you have to identify them and connect to the right resources. Make a list of everything you know you and your team could scale or become more consistent practicing. Maybe it's scaling your content distribution through your employees, or maybe it's automation software that reaches out to certain contacts once they've performed certain actions.

Now that you've got a couple of ideas, reference the Resource Library in the back of this book. Do any of these tools offer a solution that will help you become more consistent? If you're unsure, reach out to me at topofmindhelp@gmail.com or connect with your network on LinkedIn to see what tools your peers use to address similar issues.

6

BROADCASTING YOUR MESSAGE THROUGH CONTENT

Until now, we've focused more on what it means to be top of mind; how qualities like helpfulness, transparency, likability, and consistency help get you there; and content in broad strokes rather than its specific, tactical application. Understanding what it means to be top of mind is the first step; actually earning and keeping your place at the top of your audience's mind is the next.

Written content has given my company and me the fuel to nurture our networks and stay top of mind with them more easily. I want to share with you how I've done it and how you can put it into practice, too.

Before you jump to video or some other trend in communication, I can promise you this: at this moment, there is no better way to scale a top-of-mind strategy at a reasonable cost than written content. There is a time and a place for video and other similar tactics, but if you can't scale your written content now, you'll struggle with video and other tactics. You've got to walk before you can run. There is no denying these other tactics are valuable, but right now, written content remains the most scalable, affordable, and effective vehicle that should be at the core of your strategy.

The exponential rise of content marketing reflects a collective desire to reconnect with the power of the written word. Decades of exposure to relentless advertising have transformed our attention spans. As we learned to tune out ads and aggressive sales pitches, we developed a hunger for substantive, engaging information. We turned to digital content—written pieces in the form of articles, blog posts, white papers, social media posts, and so on—for knowledge, insight, and entertainment.

If you've spent more than 10 minutes reading things online within the last few years, you'll probably think my ode to content is a bit precious. I'll accept the critique; after all, the digital content landscape *is* kind of a wasteland. To pretend that humanity benefits from a thousand variations on "7 Ways to Startup Success Through Memes" would be deluded.

However, it's a wasteland only because so many people are writing content for content's sake. The explosive growth of the content marketing industry has fueled the widespread misconception that any content is good content, which is why we're drowning in "think pieces" that read like late-night infomercials.

Good content is created for the sake of the reader. Your audience comes to your content with an agenda—they want to be educated, or perhaps just entertained. Regardless, they always want to be enriched. Write to their needs and you'll earn a top-of-mind spot.

But what if you're not a great writer? What if the prospect of composing even a 600-word blog post makes you break out in sweaty dread?

If this is the case, you're not alone. I've always considered myself a lousy writer, which would be unremarkable if I weren't the CEO of one of the fastest-growing content marketing companies. Throughout the early days of Influence & Co., I was constantly nervous that

I'd be found out—I was afraid that I'd publish something poorly written, which would get me laughed out of the industry. My discomfort made me paranoid, and in time, it morphed into pretty severe anxiety about writing.

Even as the company grew by leaps and bounds, I felt like a fraud. It was only a matter of time before our competitors—or worse, our clients—discovered my lack of writing talent and everything would come crashing down. The more I suppressed my fear, the worse it got.

Finally, I couldn't take it anymore. I decided that the only way to overcome my anxiety was to come clean. I drafted a piece called "Being a Bad Writer Isn't an Excuse for Not Creating Content," in which I copped to my fear of writing and discussed my own collaborative process for writing with my team. Once the piece was finished, I almost scrapped it—the fear of publishing it was overwhelming. But my team members reminded me of the importance of authenticity and that I'd have nothing to hide—I'd feel freer. So we published it.

The post went live, and it wasn't long before several business leaders of other companies picked it up and got in touch with me. Dozens of CEOs and entrepreneurs reached out to tell me that they felt the same way and appreciated the transparency. Other leaders who said they were OK writers but didn't have the time to actually sit down and write reached out for suggestions about publishing content more consistently.

I'd been worried that the article would be embarrassing for me—instead, I felt accomplished and helpful. I learned that my problem is much more common than I'd expected. And because I talked about my own process of involving other team members to save time, I'd been able to reach a segment of my audience who felt they didn't have the time to write either. The article resonated with even more people than I thought it could.

Like me, these leaders were living in fear of being found out as mediocre writers, so it was a huge relief to discover others who were going through the same struggle. Because of this article, I was able to engage in a meaningful, emotionally vulnerable conversation with my peers. And the connections that emerged from that conversation expanded our network and made us a stronger brand.

This is why I am so passionate about content. It is a vehicle for doing everything we've discussed throughout the book so far—with good content, you can help others, provide value, and embrace transparency. All of this makes content a vital tool in your top-of-mind efforts.

How Content Gets You to Top of Mind

I've found that content is among the highest-impact ways to reach and actually connect with people in your audience and position yourself to become top of mind with them. Through quality content, you can practice and scale all of the interpersonal qualities that help you become top of mind. Through content, you can be helpful. You can educate or entertain and provide value. When you write that content yourself, you can be transparent and showcase your likability, and when you've got a good team behind you, you can keep it all going pretty consistently.

Still, in many companies, a proposal to invest in content marketing will be met with fierce executive resistance. *Why would we spend our time and money writing free articles?*

A leader who is hostile to the idea of content usually will demand hard data. *If there's no quantitative proof that content can help our business, then it's not a worthwhile investment.*

The content advocate will usually respond that content's benefits are immeasurable. *We're not going to chase vanity metrics here—you can't reduce trust and thought leadership to numbers.*

Both sides make valid points. Just as it doesn't make sense to invest in something with no demonstrable ROI, it isn't possible to quantify the emotional connections that content creates.

From a quantitative perspective, it's important to recognize that content won't generate an overnight spike in sales. That should never be the goal because that's not how content works. However, you can absolutely figure out a content proposal's breakeven points, anticipated ROI, and timetable for success. All you have to do is track the right metrics.

These include analytics such as the traffic and social shares that your content generates, as well as the amount of time visitors spend reading it or the number of leads converting from it. By measuring these, you can create monthly percentage-increase goals.

You can also measure the impact your content has on your search engine optimization (SEO) efforts by tracking search engine results page (SERP) rankings. The more content you publish, the more opportunities you generate to draw linkbacks and appear in relevant search results. This builds out more paths for your audience to connect with you and for you to stay top of mind with them.

Metrics for measuring ROI change consistently as we adopt new technology, change our goals, and learn more about our audience's wants and needs, and the ability to track these metrics is improving. Software such as Searchmetrics, Moz, SEMrush, and more (see Resource Library) can help you measure your ROI by monitoring and improving search results.

Tracking these metrics will give you tremendous insight into your audience. What topics are they most interested in? What kinds of headlines do they click on? This knowledge can guide you and your team in making constant incremental improvements to your content so that it's always relevant, helpful, and engaging.

Ultimately, though, these numbers don't tell the whole story. The real purpose of content is to build an emotional connection between you and your audience—and that's just not something you can put on a chart and present as hard evidence.

Remember, good content that's distributed correctly can position you as a credible thought leader and your company as an industry authority. It breaks down trust barriers, nurtures leads, attracts qualified candidates for hire, and invites people (within and outside of your company) to fall in love with your brand. By publishing articles and engaging your audience in meaningful conversations, you are creating real relationships with real people. Your audience may consist of only a handful of people, or it may be a network of hundreds of thousands around the world. Whatever the numbers are, content allows you to be everywhere at once—including top of mind.

And when I say everywhere, I'm not only speaking in terms of geography; I'm also talking about the past, present, and future. Good content often has an endless life span and will continue to generate interest long after you publish it—a benefit that advertising and sponsorship opportunities just don't provide. (In fact, I got a call from a reporter at a major publication seeking a quote. She had discovered me through an article I had written for *Social Media Today*—which was published years ago.)

Content offers compounding benefits. And if you constantly publish a steady stream of high-quality content, you'll be able to earn a place at the top of your audience's mind as someone who is helpful and authentic and trustworthy.

You can use that content as fuel to become top of mind with the audiences you value most, and by publishing consistently, you'll be able to keep that top-of-mind spot (and take one step closer to the content utopia I mentioned earlier).

Leaders sometimes say to me, "Isn't this a marketing function? Doesn't content fall under its umbrella?"

The short answer is yes—for now. But truthfully, these tactics can and should be used by every department, in every function of your team. My prediction is that companies will begin investing more in content across the board because these insights, knowledge, expertise, and experiences are such a core part of the company, not just the marketing department. Although marketing might act as the control center right now, the products it creates can be used to recruit talent, build investor relationships, educate current employees and keep them engaged, and more. So yes, although it's a marketing function, it needs the support of all your leaders.

Thought leadership and industry influence aren't tactics for a quick buck; they're not one-and-done plans. If you're interested in building a strong, trustworthy company brand, then authority positioning isn't a marketing-only job. It's companywide. And it starts with you.

But maybe you're not like one of those CEOs who ask me why they need to be involved. Maybe you get it. The question then becomes: How do I publish a steady stream of high-quality content when I barely have time to breathe as it is?

Creating and Executing a Content Strategy

Listen, I understand. The idea of effectively tacking on a writing career to your current leadership or management role (or adding this task to another key employee's plate) is romantic but intimidating. I can almost hear you asking, "Where will I find the time? Where will my ideas come from? What are all the resources I need to do this well?"

Relax. I've seen countless leaders (myself included) who felt at first that they would not be able to overcome these common content barriers but are now running a comprehensive strategy. If I can do it, so can you.

We all work differently. Some leaders can wake up every morning and pump out a beautifully written article as they brush their teeth. Others (myself included) need a lot more support to translate our ideas into writing—and to do it when it seems we have no time. No matter how you work, if you want to engage an audience—and you want to keep them engaged—you need to create and implement a strategy to write and distribute content consistently.

Putting a solid, responsive strategy in place is vital for achieving top-of-mind status. It ensures that you and your team are working seamlessly to create content that speaks directly to your audience. It guarantees that everything you produce will be distributed in ways that maximize its potential impact. And, most important, a good strategy infuses everything with purpose.

What follows is a brief exploration of the best practices that have proved effective for us at Influence & Co. and for many of my peers to create and distribute content to the right audience. Whether you're meeting with a potential partner or you're developing a huge communication strategy, these steps can help ensure you're engaging your audience in the right way.

Like the rest of the book, this section is meant to be a guide, not a rigid set of rules. The content landscape is too fluid and ever-changing to treat it as an exact science.

Best Practice 1: Setting the Right Goals and Documenting Your Strategy

Good content serves a purpose. It connects to the audience because it's written with them in mind. It emerges from an authentic desire to contribute to meaningful, engaging discourse. If you're always intentional about writing to fulfill a genuine purpose, you're on the path to long-term success.

Once you have an understanding of your content's core purpose, you can begin working on a plan. The planning process is an opportunity to think about your target audience, potential topics, distribution tactics, and scaling strategies. You should also be meticulous in figuring out work flows to make ideating, creating, editing, and distributing a seamless process. What will your creative ritual look like? When and how often will you create this content? Who will edit and liaise with external distribution channels?

Now, it may be tempting to talk through all of your goals and processes in broad terms and then immediately dive into creating content; after all, you're probably eager to start writing, so why wait?

Here's why: if you don't document your plan—and the research shows that the majority of companies choose not to—you are pre-emptively derailing your content initiative.[1] Without documentation, you may be able to stick to a publication and distribution schedule for a while, but the instant you hit a bump in the road, the content initiative will be moved to the back burner. And there it will remain until you have the time and motivation to get back on track, which rarely happens.

Not only will a documented content plan help you remain focused and committed, it will enable the rest of your team to figure out how they fit into—and benefit from—the initiative. And widespread internal buy-in will help integrate a love of great content into company culture.

I worked with a company whose leadership team was at one another's throats about what they should be doing, and they could not reach a decision. For a year, everyone had different ideas about what would most benefit the company. I made a simple suggestion.

I asked, "Do you have a documented strategy?"

No answer. A few embarrassed guesses that maybe marketing kind of had something?

So I took a look, made a few adjustments, and put a reasonable content marketing strategy in place. From there, the leaders added their own ideas about how these content efforts could help them out in their roles. The HR director pointed out that if the team had content about recruiting engineers, the HR team could use it to attract the right talent. The CEO brought up that certain major sites such as *Harvard Business Review* and *Forbes* would require more specific messaging. The CFO volunteered some extra budget that could be used to help other departments.

I'm not saying this went perfectly, but honestly, the result was a content strategy that reflected the goals of the entire company—not just marketing. Now, marketing took over from there, but the team anticipated tasks for which they'd need to loop in other departments, and they documented that, too. If you want a chance at being successful at executing a strategy, it's got to be written down—the big picture and the smaller to-do items. Some might argue that documenting every task that's to be completed is micromanaging; it's not.

By listing tasks and assignments for team members to complete, you're not exerting control over every step and detail, and you're not limiting how someone performs a task. You're just eliminating some of the burden on the brain that comes from not planning well enough before you begin an activity.[2]

Best Practice 2: Knowledge Extraction and Management

Once you have a documented plan in place, the next step is to create a process or system to extract the knowledge, insights, and experiences that, together, make for engaging content.

Often, you've got so many ideas, topics, and issues swirling around your head that it's hard to know where to start. Again, look to your audience for guidance. Remember content triggers? They're those conversations that inspire aha moments about your industry or your clients' needs. If vital knowledge is the treasure buried inside your mind, content triggers are the metal detectors that will tell you where to dig.

Here's an example. A few years ago, a potential client told me that high turnover and a shrinking talent pool were hurting her company's bottom line. So rather than investing in content marketing, they'd be focusing exclusively on recruitment.

Aha! Here was my target audience giving me direct insight into an issue that mattered deeply—all I had to do was listen. After the conversation, I sat with my team and we asked ourselves questions such as: What do we know about the talent shortage? What great articles have we read around strategic recruitment? Who are the thought leaders in this field? What ideas do we have for overcoming challenges like this one?

It was a free-flowing conversation that produced a diverse body of knowledge and ideas, and the team entered everything into our knowledge bank in meticulous detail.

I mentioned knowledge banks in Chapter 4—they're those templates, spreadsheets, or software options used to document your team's ideas. Knowledge banks are customizable because they're supposed to work specifically for your company, but when it comes to using one, there are a few general guidelines you should follow to make the most of it.

For one, you'll want to update your bank regularly. Your industry is constantly shifting, and keeping knowledge current is important for staying on top of changes and trends. Next, you always want to keep your audience in mind. Store your aha moments, consider any follow-up questions to those moments, and include that information as well.

From a logistical perspective, make sure your bank is as easy to navigate as possible. Create a clear system for uploading and organizing information that uses meaningful category names, as well as searchable tags and keywords.

Once your bank is in place, make using it second nature not only for yourself but for your entire team. Whenever there is a moment of insight, take it straight to the bank.

That's helpful for your content creation team, but a major benefit you might overlook (that is, until you experience it yourself) is how well an updated knowledge bank keeps engaging ideas top of mind for you even if you're not writing the content that comes from it.

An updated Google algorithm comes to mind when I think of how this plays out. Last year, my team had taken some information from Matt Cutts about a Google update straight to our bank to help me write an article on digital trends.

I happened to look through the bank one day, and the next thing I knew, I was on a call with a major client who asked me what I knew about this update. If this client had asked one day earlier, I would have said, "What update?" But because the trend was top of mind for me, I rattled off the information like I was some kind of Google expert.

Best Practice 3: Committing to a Process of Content Creation

Now for the fun part.

You know I don't love writing, nor did I have the time to do it all myself, so here's what I did: I surrounded myself with a team of fantastic strategists, writers, and editors. Together, we worked out a collaborative creative process for translating my ideas, insights, and experiences into engaging written content. (More details on how I write in the next chapter.)

For some people, creation is the most intimidating part of using content to stay top of mind. And because it's scary and time-consuming, I often hear some of the private sector's most powerful leaders weaseling out of their writing duties with the same sorry excuses: "My industry is boring, so my content will be, too!" "I'm a terrible writer!" "I don't have any media contacts!" and the classic, "I don't have any time!"

I've heard them all, and my response is always the same: Stop with the excuses, and get it done.[3]

What does this creative process look like? It's entirely up to you. Are you comfortable drafting pieces on your own and then handing them off to your team for edits? Or would you rather sit down with everyone, talk through an idea from the knowledge bank, and have your writers take it from there?

The right process is the one that makes creation easy, efficient, and fun for you and the team. After all, this is an opportunity to flex your creative muscles on a regular basis. Even if you loathe writing, you'll still look forward to content creation if you have a good process in place.

But a process is only as good as its people. When you're putting together your content team, be realistic about who you need and what their capabilities are. Choose people with the technical skills and creative capacity to help you create the best content possible.

You also need a team member dedicated to managing the entire content initiative. This is someone who will keep you on track in terms of following your content plan. Think of this person as your project quarterback—we'll talk through what this means in the next section.

Still, even with the best process and team in place, things will fall apart if you don't fulfill your role. Too many leaders dump the bulk of the mental work required to create content onto the shoulders of their writers. It's *your* job to provide the raw material that drives your team's creation efforts and to set the example that helps your team perform at its best.

When you don't live up to your responsibilities, you make it hard for your team to fulfill their responsibilities—and you're setting the example that content isn't a priority. But when you demonstrate that you're engaged in the process and willing to do what you can to achieve the best results, you're setting a positive, high-engagement expectation for your team as well.

Those kinds of expectations tend to predict how a team will perform. It's called the Pygmalion effect, and if you've heard of it, it was probably in the teacher-student context.[4] Students with teachers who have high expectations of them tend to outperform other students. So it stands to reason that when you set high expectations for your team, they will perform to meet those high expectations.

Every week, devote at least 30 minutes to brainstorming ideas before you meet with your team. You can do this at home, on your commute, at your desk, through conversation with trusted peers, in a sensory deprivation chamber—just do it. When you're intentional and thorough with your ideas, you give your team much more to work with. Not only does this elevate your content, it reinforces your expectations and can result in more productive, effective team efforts.

Best Practice 4: Publication and Distribution

Publication and distribution play a critical role in your content initiative—even the best piece won't get you close to becoming top of mind if no one in your audience ever reads it. Unfortunately, there are still plenty of leaders who pump out great content and then just let it collect digital dust on their company blog. To optimize your content's ROI—and earn that top-of-mind space—you need to be strategic, assertive, and tireless in delivering it directly to your audience.

For practical insight into what this means, let's track the life cycle of "How Executive Branding Can Help You Become Less of a Narcissist," an imaginary piece you just wrote (and that I would love to read). The edits are in, and you and your team are happy, so together, you craft an e-mail to the section editor of the publication you're targeting to pitch your exclusive new content. Following that publication's contributor guidelines, you send your unique article, a respectful pitch, and a thoughtful e-mail to the editor. After some correspondence (and potential revisions and postsubmission edits), she accepts the piece, and it goes live later that month. (I'll be honest with you: this process isn't always a breeze. One of the most common problems editors in my network share with me and my company is that content from other sources tends to be too promotional or unoriginal, and even if your content meets their criteria, the timing may not work in your favor. Contributing content is not an exact science. It's based on relationships and a commitment to engaging, unique content designed for that publication's audience—not your own agenda.)

Once it's up, your content project manager—the quarterback I mentioned earlier—begins collaborating simultaneously with:

- ▲ Your social media team, who transform the key points of the article into engaging social media content and use it (in conjunction with strategic hashtags and direct mentions) to activate amplifiers for your content and increase followers. This not only provides value to your brand followers, it also drives traffic to the article and back to your company site.

- ▲ Your PR team, who include the content in pitches to entice influencers and publication contributors to source that content.

- ▲ Your SEO team, who use the right tools and software to track its performance in search and optimize your efforts to ensure that the content is showing up for the terms that draw more of the right eyes to your work.

- ▲ Your point of contact for any and all paid promotion, distribution, and amplification efforts so you can increase your chances of getting your content in front of the specific audiences you're targeting.

- ▲ Your e-mail marketing team, who incorporate the piece into your next campaign to ensure that your distribution networks stay connected to your thought leadership efforts.

- ▲ Your human resources department, who use the article as a recruitment tool and resource for educating new hires on company culture and existing employees on industry updates.

▲ Your stakeholders, investors, and other advocates, who can educate themselves about developments in your space or share it with valuable networks.

▲ Your entire staff, so that they all can share the article through their personal and professional networks and increase the article's reach. With tools such as PostBeyond, Dynamic Signal, and Hootsuite Amplify, you can run effective employee advocacy campaigns that put this content directly into your team's hands—and their social media feeds. (Side note: Your staff's personal networks usually include proud moms, so get ready for comments like "Wow, nice job, John! Remember when you were a kiddo and you'd sing that Cabbage Patch Kids song? Look how far you've come! Love, Mom!" Still, there's value—beyond humor—that families deliver in sharing your content for you, so include personal networks in your distribution, too.)

That last point about sharing with your staff is critical. By engaging a thousand employees as brand advocates, a recent IBM campaign generated 120 million digital impressions and 141,000 clicks.[5] Even if your team is a fraction of that size, employee advocacy tools can help your team leverage their networks and achieve dramatic results.

And that's just Round 1.

If your piece hits its goals, you'll want to repurpose it for distribution through different channels (maybe even a book). Doing so will extend the life of the article and provide optimal mileage. Remember, the more opportunities you create for your target audience to connect with the piece, the greater the impact and your chances of becoming top of mind.

After it's live, republish the article on your LinkedIn page, tweaking it so that there's a direct call to action for readers to engage further with your content. Follow the comments and feedback that your piece is generating. Take note of what people are saying: What resonates with readers? What questions keep popping up? Where is the negative feedback focused?

Send the article to a handful of industry influencers, business leads, or other valuable connections and encourage members of your team to do the same. Many of the most well-connected people I know have used this tactic to build their networks, and it's one that's worked for me, too.

"I'm going to write about this topic again," you tell each of them individually. "What are your thoughts? I'd love to incorporate a quote from you."

Equipped with insight into reader response and several quotes from influencers, you and your team can rework the piece. Although the rewrite should be thorough, you're not starting from scratch; it shouldn't take as much time as the original creation process.

You now have an engaging follow-up piece on your hands.

You can repeat this process as many times as needed to create versions of the piece tailored to all of your relevant target publications, as well as your company blog. (Some caveats: obviously, avoid plagiarizing yourself and blatant redundancy.)

Finally, distill the essence of your article into different formats. These might include SlideShare decks, infographics, and white papers—the more shareable, the better. The goal is to open up new routes for your audience to discover and make use of your content.

The distribution tactics you have at your disposal are always evolving, and if you're serious about making absolutely sure that you're not only maximizing ROI but also getting your content in front of the right audiences, you've got to stay up to date with the evolution.[6]

As you can see, you can't be passive about distribution. By taking advantage of these new and creative ways to share your content with the world, you can help ensure that it gets to the right people.

Content is a powerful way to connect with those who matter most to you and to put yourself on top of their minds. It's also a wonderful tool for personal development. I recently asked a client about the benefits she had seen from investing in a content program; she told me that regularly engaging in the creative process is like working with the best leadership coach she's ever had. Through content, she's learned to open herself up to her team and rely on their guidance and feedback, which has brought them closer together than ever. Many leaders spend money on coaches or masterminds when in reality sometimes the best coach you can have is yourself.

I'm familiar with these intangible benefits because I have experienced them myself. Having worked with my team on so many hundreds of articles, I can proudly say that I'm over my writing anxiety. In fact, I now find writing therapeutic, and I make time for it every few days as a vehicle for organizing my thoughts. This was a breakthrough for me, one that continues to give me confidence and joy—and helps me stay top of mind.

7

MY JOURNEY

THE RECEPTIONIST LOOKS at me with a mixture of pity and impatience. I know what he's thinking. It's basically written on his face: *What are you, like, in high school? You're about to get eaten alive; do you even know that?*

"They're ready for you," he says with a sigh. "Come on back."

He walks me through the office without saying a word. Few people notice me, but those who do eye me with suspicion. *That kid's not really on his way to the boardroom, is he?*

As we approach the room, I can hear a loud, lively conversation coming from inside. *You're not intimidated*, I tell myself. *You're a great communicator, and you deserve to be here.* There's laughter coming from behind the closed doors. The receptionist pushes them open, and a sudden silence sweeps through the room.

Just focus on the opportunity, I think as I step inside, my mouth screwed into a smile. I greet my audience, a group of real estate leaders, the youngest of whom is twice my age. My enthusiasm is met with restrained politeness and watch-checking. With a deep breath, I launch into the background behind the project.

Just who does this kid think he is?

Would he have even been born by the time I started here?

At least he's earnest. Why can't my granddaughter ever date a boy like him?

I could tell these questions were on their minds. I was 25 at the time, and I can still feel the intense frustration of not being able to shift the spotlight from my age to my knowledge about the project or the industry in general. This was a constant struggle for me throughout my career in real estate. Many senior-level execs wouldn't give me the time of day, and it drove me up the wall. I could accept the fact that trust barriers were an inevitable part of the game, but it seemed as if all of my energy was devoted to disarming concerns about my age rather than my expertise in residential housing.

Whether you currently are or once were a young professional, I know you understand that frustration. You're more than your age, and you know that—but convincing someone else, someone older, is challenging.

The truth is that those trust barriers don't just dissolve when you're older. You aren't necessarily more trustworthy just as a result of reaching your thirtieth birthday. Whether you're pitching to a tough executive crowd or you're reaching out to candidates for a job at your amazingly successful company, your audience needs to know who you are to trust you. And your brand is a solid way to show them who you are.

I say "who you are" because that's more important and longer-lasting than "what you do" or "where you work." You could start a business, make bank, and earn a reputation in your niche as being good at what you do. But what if what you do changes? What if you built your public identity as the go-to guy for X, and then Y comes along and knocks you on your butt? Or what if you decide to change careers? Without a professional brand, it's going to be very difficult to maintain the trust you have built or transfer it to your next venture.

But at the time I noticed these trust barriers in my real estate experiences, I had never written about my industry. I didn't even have a LinkedIn profile. I'm not sure what would have come up if you'd Googled me, but I doubt it would have inspired much confidence in me as a real estate leader.

When we started Influence & Co., not much had changed. As I mentioned earlier in this book, some of those early conferences were devastating experiences for me. First of all, I often had to plead my way into getting an invite, which was always a demoralizing initial step. Of course, even when an organizer would extend an invitation (begrudgingly, I'm sure), I'd still have to pay thousands of dollars to attend. I'd show up and be a nervous wreck because I was convinced that the event would be worthwhile only if I could connect to whatever industry leader happened to be there. So after the keynote, I'd frantically elbow my way through the crowd of equally frazzled business leaders. On the off chance that I did get some face time with an industry leader, it would last for about 30 seconds, 29 of which consisted of me begging to be trusted.

The whole thing felt so isolating and impersonal. I started a business because I was confident in my ability to connect with people, but if I couldn't connect, what the hell was I doing with my life?

At one particularly miserable conference, I just couldn't muster the energy to grapple with the post-keynote crowd, so I observed from the sidelines instead. I watched as the swarm of desperate entrepreneurs descended upon the leader who had given the talk. It was as if she were on one of those moving walkways—even as she doled out face time in 30-second increments, she never stopped moving toward the door.

Finally, she got to the exit, where she was greeted by three people. She looked not only relieved but thrilled. "It's so good to finally meet you!" I heard her exclaim.

Now, I recognized these three people—they weren't Fortune 100 founders; they were young professionals like myself. I couldn't believe it. Why wasn't the speaker giving them the airport walkway treatment, too? What made these three so special?

Instinctively, I took out my phone and did some bitter Googling. I was immediately impressed—each of the three CEOs had immaculate results pages. (If you'd Googled me at that point, you'd have had to sift through a ton of stuff about the dozens of English footballers who share my name.)

I checked out their Twitter feeds, which were all packed with lessons, insights, and reactions from the keynote we had just heard. I snooped on their LinkedIn pages, which read like fascinating, bite-sized professional autobiographies. And I browsed some of the hundreds of articles each had published in top-tier industry publications. Everything I read made me want to read more.

And then it hit me. Here I was, a digital content evangelist, preaching the necessity of executive branding to anyone who would listen, but my own brand was almost nonexistent.

The truth is, at the time, I thought personal branding was inherently egotistical—which tells you what I thought about our clients. I didn't truly believe that it was necessary for growing our business. So I had never tweeted (pretty sure my avatar was still an egg) and never finished filling out my LinkedIn profile, and the few pieces I had written were buried on our then-readerless company blog.

Until that point, I had been kind of proud of my minimal footprint online; in an age of narcissistic oversharing, I was demonstrating restraint and humility. But in that moment I realized that I was actually failing as a leader. In an industry in which trust was incredibly scarce, I wasn't giving anyone a reason to trust me or my company. To treat executive branding as if it were beneath me was hurting my entire team.

After I'd come to that realization, I immediately called Kelsey. In a frantic mess of jumbled words, I explained that we really needed to practice what we preach and invest in our executive brand as our clients were doing. She agreed, and we soon started working on a creative process for developing a robust, thriving presence in the industry.[1]

Developing a Creative Process

Maria Popova has a slight obsession with the habits and routines of her favorite writers. She documents them on her website, Brain Pickings, and it's pretty fascinating. William Gibson channels his creative spirit by mowing the lawn. Kurt Vonnegut took frequent breaks from writing to do push-ups and sit-ups. Ernest Hemingway would always write standing up.

Whenever I read about a great writer's creative process, I immediately conclude that I need to do the exact same thing. And then I'll realize that although drinking a fifth of bourbon and betting on the ponies every day worked exceptionally well for Charles Bukowski, I'm not Charles Bukowski.

I've come to my process after several years of experimentation, and it works for me because it plays to my strengths, personality, and situation. Your ideal process may be completely different; what matters is that it works for you and that your final product provides value to your audience.

Research and Ideation

I recently spoke to a midmarket company that was prepared to hire an outside firm to conduct a massive research project to gather data from its customers. I'm not against hiring companies like Accenture or others to help with research. There is a time and a place for that kind of arrangement—but an internal system for documenting content triggers can help your team collect insight and data directly from your audience through everyday conversations and interactions before you outsource to another company.

Personally, my best content begins with extensive and in-depth research that my team and I conduct ourselves. I firmly believe that the best researchers are those on the front lines who are speaking to potential customers and current customers.

My concept of research is not holing myself up in a corner of the library for days on end or asking my team to work with an outside research company. Rather, research happens in conversation with clients, partners, peers, and friends. Every interaction is an opportunity to gain insight into my target audience's goals, concerns, and pain points—in other words, precisely what they want to read about.

This is what makes members of your sales team, human resources department, or client service teams such natural researchers. If you'd like to communicate with your audience of prospective customers, your sales team will know exactly what you're looking for—what kinds of questions do they always have, and what exact problems are they looking to you to solve? With that info, you can (and absolutely should) create content about those topics.

The same goes for your recruits or current clients. What kinds of conversations is your HR director having with candidates? How can your content speak to their concerns or attract the most qualified people? Your client service teams are in constant communication with current clients, which makes them the perfect researchers for that particular audience.

I was recently talking to a partner who was struggling to attract investors to his company. I asked him about the content he was publishing: Was it doing enough to convince investors that they should trust him with their money? No, this partner told me somewhat sheepishly—he actually hadn't even considered investors to be part of his target audience. Shocked, I launched into an impromptu lesson on how to create a stream of content aimed at establishing direct, robust connections between his company and the investment community.

Aha! This conversation was an obvious content trigger. So as soon as we finished talking, I sat down and typed out everything I had just said in bullet point form. I labeled the note "How to Differentiate Yourself Through Content and Attract Investors"—a clunky title, but that didn't matter. The important thing was that I now had the foundation for an article that my audience would find immediately valuable.

This is why I consider it so important to do my own research and use the data my team collects through their research in our content. By thinking of ourselves as researchers, we're always pushing ourselves to be conscious, intentional listeners—especially in personal interactions with our target audience. Not only does this equip me with insight into how to enhance the lives of the people who read my content, it also makes me a more attentive leader.

Creation

Once the research is in, it's time to create. My next step is to do what my team and I eloquently call a "brain dump," which consists of me transferring all of my knowledge and thoughts on the article topic into a document. I pay no attention to spelling, grammar, or readability. The goal is to get a stream of consciousness going so that my writing team and I have as much source material to work with as possible.

When I began doing brain dumps, I knew I wasn't constrained by the formalities of proper writing, but I still found it difficult to channel my knowledge onto the page. And then I tried to do one on a plane. I was on a flight home from a conference, and I was coming up against a publisher's deadline. So I ordered a beer, took out my iPad, and started typing out my thoughts. Without any distractions—no Wi-Fi, no e-mails, no coworkers—I got into an easy, leisurely flow. Before long, the words were pouring out of me, and by the end of the flight I knew I had found my magic writing spot.

So now my account team schedules brain dumps around my travel schedule—most of them, at least. A flight is the perfect environment for me to write about the more rational, logical aspects of running a business. However, for pieces that are more personal—pieces in which I reveal more of myself—I need a different kind of space.

In a way, my backyard is sacred space for me. It's a haven from the chaos of everyday life, a place where I can connect with my wife, watch our daughters play, and imagine what life will be like as our little family continues to grow. Sitting in my backyard, I feel centered and connected to my family and my place in the world. In this state of mind, I can process the research I've done on a deeper, more emotional level, and it becomes much easier to write about dreams, beliefs, and insecurities.

Whether I write out my thoughts in the air or in my yard, the next step is to share it with my writing team. This is where the real collaboration happens.

Once they have the brain dump, they shape the source material into a cohesive, engaging piece. Now, if I didn't trust my writers and editors, the prospect of handing off my intimate, unedited thoughts would be nerve-racking—it'd be like standing in front of the class and reading my diary out loud.

Fortunately, I trust my team; they're some of the most talented people I have ever met. It's a beautiful partnership—I bring my leadership experiences and expertise to the table, and they bring an ability to tell exceptional stories and distribute those stories to the right people. Using our goals for the piece and the publication guidelines as a creative foundation, they transform my brain dump into an article that captures my voice and perspective.

When you're working with a content team—whether it's your internal marketing department or an agency you've hired to help— there are two rules for creating engaging content. First, your company needs to do everything it can to develop a strong knowledge bank over time with content from key employees or to create a simple process to extract information consistently. In other words, you can't just hire out the entire process or rely exclusively on a series of ghost-writers—if you're not present, your voice will be lost, and you'll risk damaging your brand. Second, nothing should be published without your final approval. This is a crucial step that too many leaders neglect. You need to be aware of everything your name is attached to—always.

But here's a secret about this review and approval process: you have to be OK with some imperfections. If you go after every word and break down every comment, you'll spend way more of your time than you need to.

When I review content, I look at a couple of things. I ask myself, "Does this make sense?" and "Could anything in here hurt my brand?"

I've learned that writing is subjective, and everyone has an opinion on each point. But in reality, my job is to provide the core message and general direction of the content, and my team's is to make it consumable to my audience.

When my team has a draft, they send it to me for feedback. And let me tell you, I am not shy about sharing my honest reaction—my team is too talented to be patronized with false praise. Besides, we all share the same goal. Each of us wants to build the most vibrant connection to our readers possible. To do so, we need to work together until the piece is the best it can be.

Once the piece is ready to go live, my team submits it for publication. Even after publishing hundreds of articles in more than 50 publications, getting the e-mail from the team that something is published never gets old.

Distribution

When the piece is up, my content manager plays quarterback. She immediately throws it to our people in charge of social media and e-mail marketing, who distill the key points into shareable posts, tweets, and newsletter content. She also hits HR and sales; together, they discuss strategies for using the piece to attract talent and nurture sales leads.

On my end, I'll personally share the piece with anyone I think should read it. This usually means posting it to LinkedIn groups that are centered on relevant interests. My sales team and I have also been known to e-mail a piece directly to hot leads—doing this can help bring them closer to a purchasing decision not only by educating them on an issue but also by providing them insight into who we are as a company.

I honestly can't reiterate enough how critical this step of the process is. The best, most perfectly produced content in the world doesn't mean a thing if no one in your audience reads it.

The Impact

Once I got a team and process in place, I was able to start publishing engaging content fairly regularly. I also began to take my social media presence seriously and quickly found a lot of traction on LinkedIn. After just a few months, it was obvious that the trust barriers that had seemed so insurmountable were beginning to crumble. I was amazed. I wasn't just some anonymous schmuck anymore—I had a name and a voice now, and people were interested in what I had to say. I had created a scalable, systematic process that put me on top of a lot of industry minds.

As exciting and humbling as it was (and still is), this is where things get tricky. Here was this great aha moment when I realized that my content efforts had led to a level of influence that gave me actual authority—and that authority can be dangerous if you aren't careful and committed to authenticity.

Once you've achieved a certain level of authority, what you say almost doesn't even matter anymore because all people care about is who you are. I didn't want that for myself, and I didn't want to abuse that authority bias. I wanted my content to be why I stayed an authority.

My friend Tyler Farnsworth runs the BOLO Conference, and when he introduced me as a speaker at his event last year, he said, "Now this guy, John Hall, has been on my mind more than anyone else this year."

You might think that wording a little weird, but I consider it a great compliment. He went on to talk about how every few weeks when he's reading a trade publication or checking his social feeds, he finds something authored by me or another influencer who referenced my content. That's because of my process, and it works on many levels.

Today, I can set up a meeting with pretty much anyone in the industry. I'm invited to speak at the conferences that used to charge me thousands of dollars to attend. Brands that wouldn't give me the time of day four years ago now reach out to me for help. I'm not sharing this to brag (the transformation is still a bit surreal for me, and my wife brings me back down to earth)—this is all proof of the power of content. My content has positioned me on top of a lot of industry minds, which has created huge opportunities for both me and my company. (I've even seen my employees who use similar tactics break down more barriers.) Without this written, published content to fuel my top-of-mind strategy, I don't know where I'd be.

To stay top of mind, I know that my team and I have to continue to produce and distribute content that people find engaging and useful. I'm thankful that I have such a great team helping me do just that.

8

THE GOLDEN RULE OF COMMUNICATION

SOMETIMES WHAT YOU have to say and how you say it matter less than why you're communicating in the first place. Your job then becomes to identify why and clearly relay it to your audience to compel them to take some kind of action.

Consider the following two calls for funding:

1. The American Red Cross provides services in five key areas: disaster relief, support for America's military families, blood donations, health and safety training, and international humanitarian work. Donate today to sustain the vital work that we do.

or

2. The American Red Cross exists to provide compassionate care to those in need. Our network of generous donors, volunteers, and employees share a mission of preventing and relieving suffering, here at home and around the world,

through five key service areas. With your help, we will work toward a world in which everyone can live a full, healthy, and vibrant life.

Which one makes you reach for your wallet?

Number 1 is nothing if not informative. Reading it gives you a solid overview of the Red Cross's program areas. If you already care deeply about any of these areas or if you're already a longtime Red Cross donor, this could motivate you to make a donation.

However, most readers will find Number 2 infinitely more compelling. The language is richer—phrases such as "compassionate care," "preventing and relieving suffering," and "full, healthy, and vibrant life" grab you on an emotional level. Emotionally charged language can go a long way in establishing connections to potential donors.

Number 2's real power, though, is rooted in something deeper than word choice.

Whereas Number 1 tells the reader *what* the Red Cross does, Number 2 talks about *why* the Red Cross exists. And building your message around the *why* is absolutely vital for effective communication. As Simon Sinek explains in his fantastic TEDx Talk, "How Great Leaders Inspire Action," "People don't buy what you do; people buy why you do it."[1]

Sinek represents this concept with a simple visual diagram.[2] He draws three concentric circles. The outermost ring he labels the *what*: What do you do? What kind of products do you sell? What services do you provide? The second ring is the *how*: How do you do this? How do you create and deliver your products or services?

The innermost ring—which Sinek calls the golden circle—is the *why*: Why do you exist? What purpose do you serve? What do you believe in?

Clearly, the *what* and the *how* are important. Without a well-executed and accessible product, you won't be able to compete. That's why plenty of companies attempt to win over consumers by presenting their product or service as the best on the market. After all, doesn't the best always win out in the end?

This is logical, but it's misguided. Sinek argues that the *what* is merely a product of the *why*. You don't exist exclusively to make the product; you make the product because it is a manifestation of your core purpose. So even if you do have the best product on the market, starting with the *what* will severely restrict the connection your audience can make to your brand. You're effectively saying to your customers, "By consuming our product, you're engaging in the deepest possible relationship with our brand."

Therefore, in communicating with your audience, it's crucial that you start with *why* rather than *what*. By centering your *why*, you are opening up the core of your being to the world. You are inviting people to forge a fundamental human connection to your purpose and vision. You're saying to your audience, "Together, we can create something radically meaningful."

What Is the What?

The choice to open this chapter with an example from the nonprofit world is an intentional one.

Ask a random sampling of private sector executives why their companies exist, and most will tell you that their core purpose is to maximize shareholder wealth. As I've already explained, this is a fundamental misunderstanding of the concept of core purpose, and it's to blame for a lot of ill in the world. When profit is your primary and exclusive motivation, you're capable of doing some terrible things.

The nonprofit sector, in contrast, is explicitly cause-driven. NGOs link their existence to their missions and visions. That's why many executive directors will tell you that their goal is to put themselves out of a job because that would mean that the organization had fulfilled everything it existed to do.

This selfless focus on purpose is at the core of great communication. When you center the *why*, you aren't pushing a sales agenda onto your audience; rather, you're engaging your reader in a way that aligns with your mission.

Unfortunately, this is rare. According to one study, 75 percent of marketers use product mentions as a regular component of their content strategies.[3] This means that the vast majority of marketers still see content as a platform for brazen self-promotion rather than as a vehicle for establishing meaningful connections with the audience.

To treat content like traditional advertising is to start from the *what* because it privileges your company's desire to sell its products over your readers' desire to learn something meaningful. But at least with advertising, consumers know they're being sold to—if your content is overly promotional, your audience will likely feel that you are trying to trick them.

That's not to say that any time you mention your product you're subjecting your audience to a ruthless sales pitch. In fact, there are times when a well-placed mention can be relevant, appropriate, and beneficial to the story you're telling.

So where is the line between the *what* and the *why* in content? It can be a tough one to figure out. There are a few dead giveaways, however. Content that begins with a pitch, focuses primarily on the features of a product that the author is selling, and generates minimal social shares is probably *what*-driven. Nobody is going to spend valuable time reading this kind of content.

Here's a quick checklist for identifying content built around the *why*:

1. Does it offer substantive insight into issues and topics other than the highlights of your product?
2. Does it provide the reader actionable tips and analysis?

If the answer to both is yes, good—you're probably not stuck in the *what*. Unfortunately, that doesn't guarantee that you're in the *why*.

Why the Why Works

In his TEDx Talk, Sinek points to Apple as an example of a company that starts from the *why*:

> If Apple were like everyone else, a marketing message from them might sound like this: "We make great computers. They're beautifully designed, simple to use, and user-friendly. Want to buy one?"

To which you, the consumer, might respond: "Yeah, maybe. But there are so many companies designing beautiful computers out there, I'm going to have to do some major research and get back to you."

Sinek continues:

> Here's how Apple actually communicates. "Everything we do, we believe in challenging the status quo. We believe in thinking differently. The way we challenge the status quo is by making our products beautifully designed, simple to use, and user-friendly. We just happen to make great computers. Want to buy one?"

Now, for people who are apathetic about (or happy with) the status quo, the above statement won't have much resonance. However, if you believe yourself to be a critical thinker—someone who lives life with intention rather than just accepting that things have to be the way they always have been—hearing this statement will be immensely validating. Here is a company that shares the values and beliefs that you hold dear. The invitation is clear: You want to change the world, and so does Apple. Together, you may just be able to.

This is the power of starting from the *why* in your content. By foregrounding your core purpose, you can activate the deeply held beliefs and values of your target audience. This fosters a deep, identity-driven connection between your audience and your brand. When your *why* motivates your content, you're taking a principled stand—and you're inviting your audience to stand right next to you. And that kind of connection is what truly engages your audience.

To create *why*-driven content, there is a simple (if obvious) starting point. *Why?* (It's a loaded question, as we'll soon see.) Specifically, apply that *why* to the following questions: Why am I creating this content? Why does my company exist? And, most important, why do I do what I do?

Why Am I Creating This Content?

In her post "5 Powerful Rules for Women Entrepreneurs to Live By," Sumi Krishnan, the founder of K4 Solutions, says this:

> When I became an entrepreneur, I was motivated by one thing: freedom. I wanted the flexibility to follow my dream. Entrepreneurship allowed me to do work that was engaging and empowering. . . . But there's no magic formula for entrepreneurial success, of course. Stepping into the unknown is scary—and many women doubt their abilities, feeling like impostors. "I believe that no matter how thoroughly prepared a woman might be, she will feel unprepared, whereas a man will feel even more prepared than he really is," [CEO of Pearl Aqua LLC Linda] Shesto says. Unfortunately, research supports this notion. Here, then, are five strategies to help you crush these types of entrepreneurial fears and succeed even as you step into the unknown.[4]

Why did Krishnan create this content? Her purpose is crystal clear: to equip her fellow women entrepreneurs with strategies for conquering their most common fears. She knows her audience and is speaking directly to them on both an emotional and a practical level. Notice that Krishnan shifts the spotlight, making room for voices other than her own. By sharing lessons gained from personal experience—both from her life and from the lives of other women entrepreneurs—Krishnan's fundamental message to her reader is "Don't worry. You're not the only one struggling with fear. As women, we can understand, support, and nurture each other, because we're all in this together."

Krishnan is a thoughtful, emotionally intelligent writer who clearly cares about the needs of her audience. Her sense of purpose shines through in her content, and it clearly resonates with her readers. By writing to enhance the lives of her audience, Krishnan earns their trust—and for many of them, she will likely become top of mind.

Why Does My Company Exist?

Yvon Chouinard is the founder of iconic outdoor apparel company Patagonia. His reflective piece "On Corporate Responsibility for Planet Earth" opens:

> As an alpinist who set out to make gear for my friends and never thought of myself as a "businessman" until long after I became one, I've wrestled the demons of corporate responsibility for some time. Who are businesses really responsible to? Their shareholders? Their customers? Their employees? None of the above, I have finally come to believe. Fundamentally, businesses are responsible to their resource base. Without a healthy planet there are no shareholders, no customers, no employees. As the conservationist David Brower liked to say, "There is no business to be done on a dead planet."

But what does behaving responsibly to the environment mean? It took me nearly 25 years in business to learn how to ask that question. It has taken another 15 years of trial and error to uncover the process that Patagonia—or any environmentally minded company—has to go through in pursuit of answers. I think I know how to break that process down to five steps. These steps apply to individuals as well as to companies who want to reduce the harm they do and make a difference.

Reading this piece, it's immediately clear that Patagonia is, first and foremost, a group of people devoted to mitigating the impact that humans have on the natural world—they just happen to do this by selling environmentally sustainable outdoor gear. However, the piece explains that business is just one avenue for creating positive change: Chouinard argues that any company striving to be sustainable must not only reduce its environmental costs, it must also nurture civil democracy by giving direct support to frontline activists, as well as lobbying for industrywide changes toward fairness and sustainability.

Patagonia's purpose serves as an invitation for readers who are passionate about the environment to join the company in fighting for the Earth.

Why Do I Do What I Do?

My friend Dustin McKissen is the founder of McKissen + Company and one of LinkedIn's Top Voices in Management and Culture. Hilarious, devastating, and enlightening, Dustin's writing demonstrates the power of knowing yourself and your purpose. Consider this excerpt from "Five Reasons Why I'm Not Sleeping in My Car Anymore":

When I was 18 I could no longer live under the same roof with my dad (who, at the time, was mutually deciding with my mom that they could no longer live under the same roof together). I moved out with no money, no place to go, and no plan.

I moved into my Geo Tracker.

Living in a Geo Tracker is nothing if not an adventure. . . . I would often sleep in the parking lot of a gym I belonged to. I could wake up, work out, and shower. One night I forgot to lock my car and woke up because my door was open, and a man was just watching me sleep. It was alarming.

So, while I recognize the absurdity of a guy who is just a normal person writing a "How I Got Where I am Today" post, it's a long way from these stories to where I am now. . . .

This year I'll spend Thanksgiving at home for the first time in a couple of years, and that's awesome too. I'll spend it with—all due respect to Seth Godin—the only tribe that really matters to me.

I met my wife when I was 22, we got married two months later, and by 26 I had three kids, one of which was her daughter that I adopted when we got married.

Even when stuff goes seriously wrong in my career, I know the basics like love and having a home are taken care of. And by home, I don't mean our literal home (though I like having a bed). I mean a place to call home. Five people would be a lot to fit in a Geo Tracker, but even if we have to do that one day, it will still be a home in the way that my prior Geo Tracker wasn't.[5]

Why does Dustin work? Why does he write? Why does he do what he does?

"My main motivation for work, my writing, and my career choices is a desire to be heard," Dustin recently told me over e-mail.

"At one point growing up my mom supported us by working at McDonald's and earning the minimum wage, for a time we received food stamps, and at one point we lived in a tent. I know what it's like to not be heard, and that motivates why I write, and what I write about.

"And I know what I'm doing is working, and I know it because last week my son (who is 10) wrote a letter to his elementary school's administration about the lack of sportsmanship on the soccer field. He offered some solutions, and I was proud of him for caring about others and demonstrating empathy, even for the kids who were being 'bad sports.' But I was even prouder that my son felt like he had an opinion someone should listen to. He wanted to be heard, and believed he should be heard—and he beat me to that realization by 20 years."

I find Dustin's clarity and conviction inspiring. Reflecting on my own purpose, I realize that everything I do—in terms of content, leadership, and all other aspects of my life—I do for my family. My family is my purpose and my foundation, and my role as provider goes deeper (much deeper) than simply bringing home an income. I want to help my kids live up to their full potential as learners and doers, and I want to help my wife live with satisfaction and joy. I work to nurture the bonds that connect all of us to each other so that each of us knows we are part of something bigger than ourselves.

Clearly, starting from the *why* is not only a strategy for creating effective content. When you live with a sense of purpose, everything you do is infused with meaning. You're able to keep challenges in perspective, and you make intentional choices. Success becomes something intensely personal. You become connected to what matters.

It also keeps you on top of people's minds—in the right way. How do you want people to think of you when you're top of mind for them? Do you want to live in the shallow end, driven more by the *what*? Or do you agree that being top of mind in a way that clearly communicates who you are and why you do what you do is more important?

Obviously, factors such as familiarity and likability play into how people think of you. But don't for a minute think that they're not also considering your *why* when you're on top of their minds.

I'm reminded of an introduction I once got from one industry influencer to another. When he introduced me, he didn't just say, "Here's John. You should talk to him." Instead, he said that my team and I are the best at what we do: helping clients build industry influence and authority by working with them to create and distribute content.

It was something I'd struggled with myself, so I knew how important it was, and I'm committed to helping others overcome those barriers, too. And I had content out there that dived deep into who I am and why I lead this company. Together, those elements reflect my *why* and help me earn top-of-mind space.

Finding your purpose is your life's work, and it never ends. The search makes you the best person you can be, and communicating it to your audience can put you top of mind.

9

BEYOND THE
MARKETING DEPARTMENT

AT AN EVENT this year, I ran into the head of strategy for one of the country's biggest hotel chains. He was excited. As a marketer, he had long known that a major investment in his personal brand would yield benefits for both himself and his employer. He had recently brought this up in discussion with his leadership team, and everyone was in agreement. Thanks to this conversation, the company would be investing in personal branding for leaders across the entire team. The head of strategy recounted all of this beaming with pride.

At that point, everybody I knew seemed to be looking for a new job, so I asked this person how long he planned to stay with the hotel chain. His response: "They're treating me right. Why on earth would I leave?"

Same event, next day. I'm talking to another head of strategy; this one was with a major restaurant chain. She had also brought up the importance of personal branding with her team, but the response she had received was far less enthusiastic. The CMO said something to the effect of "Do whatever you like, but you're on your own in terms of funding." Understandably, this head of digital was angry.

I asked her whether she would stay with the restaurant company in the long run. Her response: "If you were me, and you always had to pay out of pocket to invest in yourself, would you stay?" By the end of the month, she had quit.

Leaders who won't fund personal branding efforts usually argue that doing so would be an unnecessary expense. And while they may well be concerned about the budget, there is often a deeper fear at play that nobody will admit to—what if we invest in our people only to have them turn around and leave us?

It's a scenario I know well. When we hired our first VP of sales, we were thrilled. He was a perfect fit for the position, and he had tremendous potential to take the company forward in the long run. We poured a ton of money, time, and energy into training him and helping him develop a thriving personal brand. He worked with us for four years, then went to work for one of our partners.

Was I disappointed? Sure. We were losing a good employee. But was I angry with this person? Not at all. I was happy for him because I genuinely cared about him, and I knew he'd be successful in his next position. In fact, we made sure that we continued to invest in his training up until his last day. And because there was never any bitterness or acrimony, he's now one of Influence & Co.'s biggest brand advocates working for one of our largest partners. He continues to create opportunity for us on a regular basis.

This experience cemented our belief that an investment in our team is an investment in our company. Recently, two of our employees decided to leave. The transition was a hard one emotionally—these people are like family, after all—but again, we were all excited to see what great things they would do next. One had secured a job at Facebook, and the other at Lyft.

From an opportunity-creation perspective, I'm so grateful to have Influence & Co. alumni advocating for us in such innovative places. And on a personal level, the pride I feel in seeing some of the world's most innovative companies hire our people is overwhelming.

Employees will leave and pursue other opportunities. Still, it's important that you don't let this prevent you from investing in them. Richard Branson once said, "Train people well enough so they can leave; treat them well enough so they don't want to." When you invest in your team, your organization becomes a place where people can become their best selves and do their best work. They benefit, you benefit, and your brand benefits long into the future.

A Team Full of Thought Leaders

Your team consists of a diverse and ever-evolving collection of perspectives, experiences, and insights. All of your team members have something valuable to say, and each of them has a trusted position within his or her own networks and social circles. In other words, every employee is a potential thought leader.

And yet so many companies restrict thought leadership efforts to the exclusive domain of the C-suite. In many cases, only one person (usually the founder or CEO) is allowed to publish content in the brand's name. The logic goes like this: if there are more than one or two voices speaking for the brand, we won't be able to control the message—and that's a scary thought. Plus, as I previously discussed, many executives are afraid that strong employee personal brands will make it easier for competitors to poach their top talent.

If you think that rigid guidelines will ensure a unified brand message, I've got news for you: your team is your brand, and your brand is your team.

Every time an employee tweets from a personal account, she is representing your company (yes, even if it says "views = my own" in her bio). Whenever your staff shares something on LinkedIn, they do so as brand representatives. There are no benefits to silencing employee voices—you only end up creating dissonant noise and making your team feel disenfranchised (which gives your competitors great leverage in their poaching efforts). What's worse, you're squelching one of your most valuable branding assets.

On average, your employees will have 10 times as many social media followers as your brand account.[1] Why wouldn't you tap into these networks?

By doing so, you can create social proof that can be extremely valuable for your brand. With a team sharing your content, your social distribution numbers will be much larger, and that network can create a domino effect of positive recognition and social proof from users and influencers who interact with it. As I said, social activity and engagement with content is a lot like saying, "I endorse this message," even if a bio claims otherwise. When that person's followers see your content, they'll be more inclined to engage, too.

Remember, your team members occupy the intersection between your brand and the outside world. This puts them in the best position to educate current clients, prospects, and future employees about your culture. If you nurture your employees' individual abilities to communicate the essence of your brand, their voices will come together in a harmonious way.

Think of it as if you're conducting a choir—every voice adds depth, nuance, and power. By creating a culture of democratic thought leadership, you can ensure that every team interaction with leads, partners, recruits, and the public will be enriching and inspiring. And for many employees, adding value throughout networks can be a major source of pride. As we saw in the beginning of the chapter, when your employees feel a profound emotional connection to the company, they're much more inclined to stick around.

Turning your team into an army of thought leaders has a profound positive impact on your audience, as well. Audiences now hold different attitudes about what makes brands and companies authentic, and we're seeing that shift toward individualism as a form of a

brand's authenticity. Each individual member of your team con-
tributes to your brand, and the more intentional you are about empowering that contribution, the more authentic your audience will
perceive you to be.

That's because when team members speak out for your brand,
they humanize it. Suddenly your company isn't just some faceless
corporation; it's a group of real people who talk about real issues and,
in doing so, invite the audience to connect on a human level. And
the more members of your team who can connect with your audience, the more likely it is that your company will become top of mind
with them.

Breaking Down Silos with Content

Of course, it would be decidedly undemocratic to limit democratic
thought leadership to the marketing department. To truly harness
the potential of your team, you need to invest in thought leadership
across all departments.

I've previously explained how crucial other departments (such
as sales and HR) are to your content distribution efforts, as they are
positioned to deliver the content you publish directly to leads and
potential talent.

However, to engage them only after you click "publish" is to leave
some gaping holes in your content. Your audience is as diverse as
your team is, and you need to provide a window into your organization that is both broad and deep. Not only should voices and perspectives from other departments be present in the content *you* create,
other departments should be creating their own content as well.

So what is the relationship between your content initiative and
various departments? What content goals should different departments pursue, and what impact can they expect to see? And, importantly, which departments are positioned to yield the greatest

benefits—and should therefore be contributing to your content budget? Here's an overview.

Marketing

It's logical that your marketing department would serve as home base for the company's thought leadership efforts. After all, thought leadership is a communications platform for marketing the people and ideas that make your company special. Plus, your content is fuel for your other marketing efforts, from social media to e-mail campaigns. A robust thought leadership initiative can streamline, enhance, and amplify your entire marketing strategy from the ground up.

The benefits that democratic thought leadership can yield for your marketing department are immense. Having multiple thought leaders represent your company will increase brand equity exponentially. This bolsters company credibility, which in turn dissolves trust barriers, invites customer loyalty, and helps generate qualified leads. There are few marketing goals that companywide thought leadership can't help you reach.

But what might a thought leader from your marketing team write about? Consider the following excerpt from "4 Ways to Jumpstart Your Content Strategy Next Quarter," a blog post by Maya Luke.

> 1. Host a Content Party. Oh, you don't have regular content parties? This is sort of a ritual every three months for our marketing team, and boy, is it a blast (mimosas may or may not be involved on occasion).
>
> Aside from all the fun and games, this meeting is absolutely necessary for us to brainstorm and outline what the next quarter of content will include and how each piece fits into our overall marketing funnel.
>
> This way, we can plan out three months of a strategy, and everyone understands from the beginning what guest-contributed

and internal content needs to be produced. Try hosting regular content parties to plan out your strategy so you can thoroughly impress your CMO with all your ideas.[2]

In this piece, Maya is speaking directly to a niche target audience—her fellow marketers working on content strategy—and the guidance she provides is as helpful as it is completely, characteristically Maya. Pieces like this helped position Maya (and Influence & Co.) on top of her readers' minds, which in turn boosted our brand equity and helped attract informed leads. (A quick note: When Maya wrote this piece, she was our director of content and social media. She now works at Lyft.)

Sales

A while back, my VP Natalie Stezovsky had a conversation with a prospect. This person had already made the decision to invest in content; now the choice was between creating it in-house and partnering with a company to manage it for him.

Rather than jumping down his throat with an aggressive pitch, Natalie forwarded to him a post I had published about in-house content teams. The piece is not some thinly veiled advertisement for our services; in it, I actively encourage readers who have the right resources to *not* hire out their content but create it in-house instead.

In sending this piece, Natalie demonstrated a desire to help. By providing relevant, objective information, she positioned herself as a trustworthy peer and not an agenda-driven salesperson. There's nothing underhanded about this because if the lead *did* have access to great in-house writing talent, his company ultimately wouldn't have been a great fit for us. Our ideal client is someone whose needs and resources align perfectly with ours—which sets the stage for the healthiest, most robust long-term relationship possible.

Constant customer interactions provide your sales team with some of the deepest insight into your target audience. What sales barriers do they struggle with? What concerns do leads have about the industry? By providing thought leadership content on these issues, your sales team can generate trust, establish valuable connections, and develop a reputation for being educators rather than predators. And that can be a tremendous help in closing sales and growing your business.

Recruitment and Training

Recently, I was chatting with a potential new hire. She seemed like a great fit right off the bat. I asked her how she'd heard about the company.

"Your content," she responded.

About a year prior, she had discovered an article by Kelsey; since then, she had read just about everything our team had published.

"When I read that first piece by Kelsey, I knew immediately that she was someone I wanted to work for. The more I read, the more excited I got about the idea of working in a place where people spoke their minds but didn't take themselves too seriously."

By the way, Kelsey's piece that had initially attracted the candidate was not called "The 6 Things You'll Love Most About Working for Influence & Co." In fact, the piece wasn't even specifically about our company—the focus was on women in tech. But reading the article gave this candidate a sense of the values and philosophy at the foundation of what we do—a sense of our *why*. As she pored through our content, she also developed a sense of who we are as people, what we care about, and how we personally view our industry. By publishing content like this consistently, we were able to stay on top of her mind. All of these things resonated with her, and they inspired her to apply the minute she saw an opening. (We hired her. Obviously.)

This is the power of content to attract top talent. High-quality, diverse thought leadership content is a portal that invites readers to step into the inner workings of your company and to connect with your values and culture.

When key employees publish bylined pieces, they humanize your brand, revealing their distinct personalities to the world. This makes it easier for potential candidates to envision themselves working with you. Remember, top talent wants to work for the best—by positioning your team and yourself as industry thought leaders, you're making your company an attractive place to be.

Content is also a means to weed out low-quality applicants. Paul Roetzer of PR20/20, for example, posts articles that are relevant to the company's current job openings on his website. When someone applies for a specific position, Roetzer tracks the applicant's activity by using marketing software. Applicants who don't bother to read the articles don't get called in for an interview. Think about it—if you publish a piece a day but the candidate sitting in front of you hasn't read anything you've written, what does this say about his level of commitment and preparedness? If he's competing with a potential hire who quotes your articles and asks in-depth questions about your content and culture, there should be no contest.

Rather than tracking if a prospective employee browses your on-site content on his or her own, consider taking an active approach by sending a candidate content throughout the application and interview process. In the final interview, you'll be able to gauge how much the candidate learned throughout the process. Intellectual curiosity is a vital trait in good employees, and this process can give you an idea of how interested candidates are in continued education.

Great content won't only help you find your dream employee—it's also a valuable training tool. When we were a team of 20 people, I would happily conduct one-on-one trainings with everyone we hired. But now that our team has grown substantially, even working across different cities, that's no longer feasible. So now we send new employees a "Before Day 1" document that includes content that my leadership team and I have published. This serves as a bridge for us to be involved in the training process from a distance. We still get to play the role of educators, helping bring new hires on board with our company culture and letting them learn about developments in the industry. Content enables us to form a meaningful connection with each employee.

Referral Programs

Referral or partner programs can span various departments, and no matter what kind you set up, a top-of-mind mindset can be extremely effective. It's easy to think about how awesome you are when you're raking in referrals, but you can't get complacent. You've got to engage consistently with your partners to take full advantage of your referral program and create opportunity for your business.

Remember all the time we spent discussing likability, helpfulness, and other trust touch points? You can implement those ideas into a referral program to connect with your audience of current partners and clients.

Let me walk you through how my team increased our referrals and what we've seen clients do, too. (You can make the necessary changes if you're switching between B2B and B2C.)

Step 1: Identify what makes a good referral partner or client partner. Before investing time and resources, identify the prospective partner as someone with a network or audience that's going to be valuable to you.

Step 2: Deliver to this person all the information he or she needs to make an introduction (personally or through your website) to your company as easy as possible.

Step 3: Consider all the trust touch points and tools you have at your disposal and brainstorm ways you can use them to engage this partner. In the past, we've offered free services, gifts, introductions, and so on, and if she's going to send any opportunity our way, she'll typically do so within the next 90 days or so. When she does, you can move away from content to begin investing more in the kinds of trust touch points that aren't as scalable and really make the experience as enjoyable and effective as possible.

Using a system like this allows you to prioritize your most valuable partners and make your relationships with them as meaningful and personalized as possible while still keeping everyone engaged with content to stay top of mind.[3]

Simple, right?

Nurturing Thought Leadership Across Your Team

Now that you understand the *why* of democratic thought leadership, it's time to look at the *how*. Fortunately, the process for positioning yourself as a thought leader runs parallel to doing so for key members of your team. It's a simple concept, after all—listen to your audience, write about what they'll find interesting, publish, distribute, and repeat.

However, as gung ho as *you* may be about the process, you may encounter a bit of resistance from the other potential thought leaders on the team. And indeed, publishing a stream of great, consistent content can sound like a daunting prospect, especially when it seems outside of a person's job description.

The words of the late, great stand-up Mitch Hedberg come to mind: "When you're a comedian, everybody wants you to do things besides comedy. They say, 'OK, you're a stand-up comedian—can you act?' It's as though if I were a cook and I worked my ass off to become a good cook, they said, 'All right, you're a cook—can you farm?'"

Some people won't understand why they should invest their time and energy into becoming thought leaders. This is a common concern, and if you don't address it fully, it can derail your entire initiative; without a solid understanding of why and an authentic buy-in, the content that the team produces will be either weak or nonexistent.

The first step is to explain how their thought leadership is important to the entire business. Explain to these key employees that as individual thought leaders, they'll be bolstering the goals and efforts of their respective departments; as a collective, they are the company's competitive advantage. Get them excited about their contributions—when they share their expertise, everyone benefits.

The next barrier you'll likely encounter is the fear of writing. As I've discussed previously, it's something that many of us struggle with. Thankfully, to become a thought leader, you don't need to be a great writer. All your teammates need to do is to supply the raw material—the ideas, insights, and expertise that are already swirling around inside their heads—and the writers will mold it into cohesive, polished content. For people with truly debilitating aversions to writing, make concessions; they can contribute through conversations, interviews, or informal e-mails. Do whatever it takes to ensure that everyone is comfortable and eager to take part.

Technology can also play a powerful role in making the process as collaborative, smooth, and painless as possible. Our team recently created our own software, Core, to help us streamline communication and create content more collaboratively. Plus, software such as 15Five and Slack allow us to crowdsource ideas and information. And remember our old friend the knowledge bank? A robust knowledge bank is a constant, reliable source of collective wisdom, which makes it a vital tool for collaboration.

Finally, make sure that everyone understands the personal benefits of the initiative. Being a thought leader dissolves barriers and positions you on top of the minds you care about. This helps you do your job more efficiently and effectively, and it improves your career prospects. By investing in themselves and their personal brands, your teammates are investing in the entire company.

10

POPULATING ALL STAGES OF THE CONSUMER JOURNEY THROUGH STRATEGIC DISTRIBUTION

BEN IS A FRIEND of mine with a six-month-old daughter named Yatri. Since the day Yatri was born, it has been clear to Ben and his wife, Michele, that their baby is a creative genius—she is alert, curious, and an extremely articulate babbler. Naturally, Ben and Michele want to provide Yatri every opportunity to nurture her creative potential. And so, even though their child is only six months old, Ben and Michele have begun searching for the perfect preschool.

Although they don't remember much from their own preschool days, Michele and Ben know that they want Yatri to be in a learning environment where she'll be encouraged to think critically and independently. They also want her to learn about the world through diverse cultural perspectives as well as to establish a meaningful connection to nature. Science, music, and literature are very important to both parents, and they believe these should be central to Yatri's education.

Equipped with these fundamental requirements, the parents set out to learn everything they can about early childhood education. Their quest for knowledge begins (as most do) with a period of intense Googling. What kinds of schools are out there; which one would be best for Yatri? Are there public options that would fit their needs, or will they need to go the private route? And finally, will they have to take out a second mortgage just to put Yatri through preschool?

Their search yields hundreds of online articles, think pieces, and videos. A lot of what comes up are ads for private schools that are poorly disguised as helpful content; Ben and Michele dismiss these without a second thought. But they do encounter a few insightful pieces that capture their attention.

One stands out in particular: "Making Sense of Pre-School." This piece was published on a local parenting site, and it provides a concise, accessible overview. The author, Annabel Bruno, explains major alternative educational philosophies, answers questions about the private versus public debate, and touches on common concerns over tuition. The information is so useful that the piece becomes Ben and Michele's cheat sheet.

After about two weeks of research, Michele and Ben develop a basic but solid understanding of the options available to them, and they find themselves leaning toward the Waldorf style of education.

More Googling produces more articles—and once again, they encounter a great Annabel Bruno piece: "How to Choose a Waldorf School That's Right for You." Annabel's guidance is so relevant and on-point, it's as if she's right there with them. Ben and Michele check out Annabel's Twitter feed, where they learn that she is the founder of a Waldorf school, the New Toronto Waldorf Academy. They follow the link to the school's website and pore through its excellent blog. One of the posts has a link to gated content called "Preparing Your Family for Waldorf"; Michele happily enters her e-mail address to receive it. She and Ben read through the document together and talk about it throughout the evening.

A few days later, Michele gets an e-mail from Annabel: "I really hope you've found our materials useful, Michele. It can be such a daunting prospect to start thinking about preschool. If you'd like, we can set up a time to talk through some of your questions. In the meantime, here are a few more resources that you might like."

Included in the e-mail is a link to an article by Mischa Berlin, Annabel's tech director, about the role of technology in alternative education. This is particularly interesting to Michele and Ben, who have been wondering how they can help Yatri foster a healthy relationship with technology as she gets older.

Over the course of the next year, Annabel remains top of mind for Michele and Ben. How could she not? They follow her on social media, read everything she publishes, and receive her newsletter. The school's blog has provided an honest glimpse into what sets its preschool apart from the competition. When Yatri turns a year and a half, Ben and Michele get a personal invitation from Annabel to submit an application, along with a video showcasing the highlights of the preschool. By the time she's two, Yatri is a proud student at the New Toronto Waldorf Academy.

Every Step of the Journey

Michele and Ben's story is a perfect case study in the power of content to connect with the buyer at every stage of the journey. I use the term *buyer* because we're all familiar with the buyer's journey—not because the practices are limited to literal buyers. The same ideas apply to any audience, regardless of the intent to purchase.

If you're a recruiter, for example, this can be adapted to your target candidate. The journey that a person takes to your company follows the same phases, and content can influence that journey in much the same way. The strategies outlined are relevant across the board.

For your target buyer (or target employee, target partner, target investor, etc.), the path to your company is a journey. It begins with a need, problem, or desire, which sparks a quest for knowledge. Throughout this process of self-education, your target buyer will encounter the various options that are available to her, which will inevitably include whatever your competition is offering. By proving yourself to be a helpful, trustworthy resource throughout the learning experience, you can help her connect the dots between her need and your company. If she sees a fit, you'll close the deal.

Notice how the nature of Annabel's content shifted as the young parents got closer to their purchasing decision. Initially, Ben and Michele simply needed to know what their options were; "Making Sense of Pre-School" helped them do just that. When they began to narrow their focus, Annabel's content got more context-specific (note that *specific* does not mean *overly promotional*; Annabel was still positioning herself as a trusted expert rather than pushing an aggressive sales agenda). Only when Ben and Michele were ready to make a decision did Annabel begin her pitch, and because she had used content to position herself on top of their minds as a trustworthy resource, their decision was easy.

You can see that it's not enough to create great content—you have to create great content that targets your audience's needs in the moment. To do this, you have to completely understand each stage of their journey. Once you know how they move through these various stages, you can create a funnel around the journey so that their path leads to you.

On average, the buyer's journey provides an opportunity for 30 potential touch points to connect with your prospect. The more of these you hit, the greater your chances of remaining top of mind. And content is the most efficient, scalable way to hit as many of those touch points as possible.

Here's how the journey unfolds and some insight into strategies for using content to stay top of mind at every stage, which will help move your audience through the funnel toward your company (Figure 10.1).

Figure 10.1 **Content Marketing Funnel**

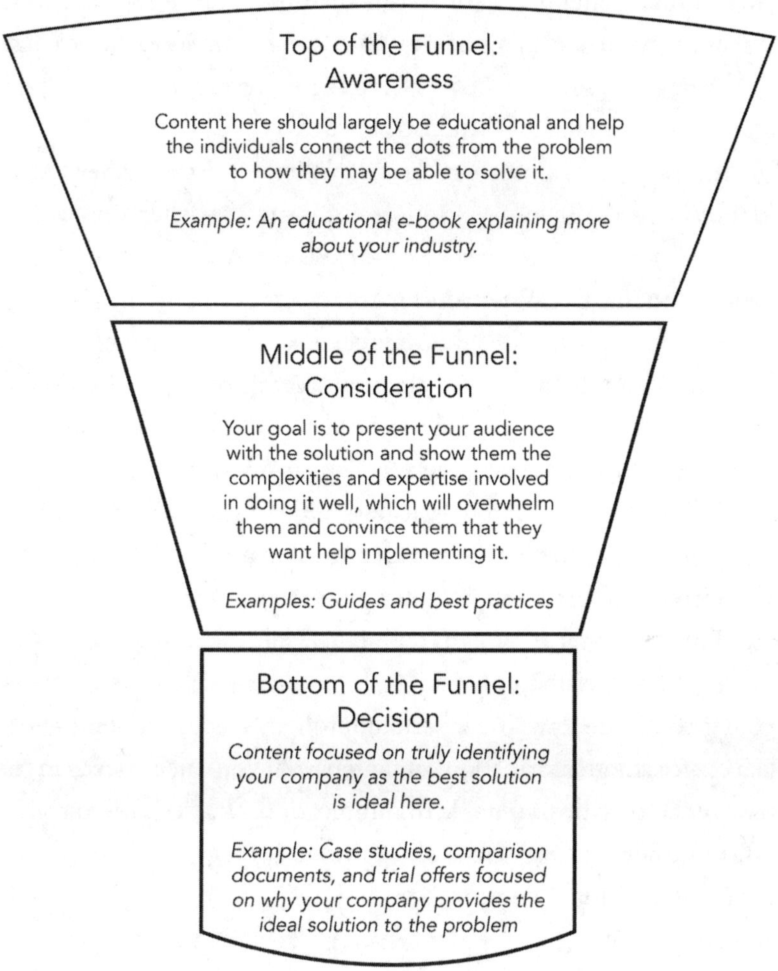

Top of the Funnel:
Awareness

Content here should largely be educational and help
the individuals connect the dots from the problem
to how they may be able to solve it.

*Example: An educational e-book explaining more
about your industry.*

Middle of the Funnel:
Consideration

Your goal is to present your audience
with the solution and show them the
complexities and expertise involved
in doing it well, which will overwhelm
them and convince them that they
want help implementing it.

Examples: Guides and best practices

Bottom of the Funnel:
Decision

*Content focused on truly identifying
your company as the best solution
is ideal here.*

*Example: Case studies, comparison
documents, and trial offers focused
on why your company provides the
ideal solution to the problem*

Problem Identification and Awareness

The journey begins when the buyer becomes aware of a specific problem, opportunity, or need that she's facing. Her primary need right now is information: What are the options? How can she fulfill this need or address this problem? What are the experiences of others in this situation? What challenges can she expect to face as she moves forward?

During the problem identification stage, the distance between your buyer and her purchasing decision is the greatest it can be. This makes many professionals panic—*if we don't hook 'em early, we'll lose them forever!*—and their anxiety leads them to create shallow content that reads like spam.

If you try to manipulate or deceive your target buyer in her search for objective, useful information, you really will lose her forever. But if you prove yourself to be a credible expert, you can create an initial connection that could span the length of the journey.

Remember how Ben and Michele discovered Annabel's article on a parenting site they already trusted? At this point, your prospective customers don't necessarily know who you are. The chances that they'll visit your site right away are virtually nonexistent.

That's why it's so important to leverage third-party credibility into your own. Find out where your target buyers "live" online. What publications do they read? What social media platforms are they using? Publish content through (and specifically for) those channels.

You also need to implement calls to action that direct visitors to your gated content where you can offer them even more value in exchange for some information on their part. If you can get your target buyer to subscribe to e-mail communications, the long-term possibility of conversion skyrockets. Your gated content, therefore, has to provide exceptional value.

The goal with gated content is always to create mutual benefit—your readers get premium access to relevant insight, and you enter valuable information into your database, taking you a step closer to becoming top of mind.

Research and Consideration

The research stage is often the lengthiest of the entire journey, which is why most of your content will be targeted here. Because your audience has so much information to sift through and process, you need to be patient, strategic, and, perhaps most important, consistent. The greater the quantity of tactical, actionable, educational content you publish, the better your chances of staying top of mind throughout what may be a long process.

At this point, you've already helped your audience identify key problems and opportunities; now it's time to explore solutions.

Your goal at this stage is to nurture your best leads through the middle of the funnel. To do this, you need to create content that is slightly more company-oriented—focused on your products and services if you're selling or your company culture if you're recruiting. Remember, though, that the focus needs to remain squarely on the needs of your audience—you're an educator, not a salesperson. If the audience feels that you gained their initial trust only to turn around and bombard them with advertising, they'll drop you quickly.

Although it's still important to leverage credibility from third-party publications, you also want to encourage your audience to spend more time on your website. Through onsite content, you can further establish yourself as a valuable resource on the buyer journey. And in educating your target audience as they do their research, you'll demonstrate the way in which you create value—an attractive prospect when thinking about future purchasing decisions.

Decision Making

In the final stage, your audience has developed a pretty thorough understanding of their problem and the potential solutions that are available. They're now ready to begin evaluating options and make a decision.

By this point, your audience is well aware of your agenda. Still, your job as a thought leader is to remain a trusted resource—if they feel that you don't have their best interests at heart, you'll lose credibility, which could cost you the relationship.

Help them weigh the pros and cons of their various options; continue to answer their most pressing questions. Back up the information you provide with empirical evidence—what have others done in the past? How did it work out?

Use your content to make a strong, evidence-based case for your company. If you're really the best option, explain why. Create comparison guides that make the advantages you offer over the competition crystal clear and comprehensive content that addresses any remaining concerns your audience might have at this point.

If you're selling your services, this is the point where your sales team enters the picture, and it's important that they're ready to leverage the content as a tool for closing the deal. If you're recruiting talent, this is where your HR director comes in to make sure the candidates you've attracted with your content are qualified and a good fit for your company.

Whatever your goal is, make sure your team understands the direct relationship between thought leadership and conversion. Everyone is working toward the same goal, so be sure that communication among team members remains open and honest.

Good content in this final stage communicates urgency, differentiates your company and what you offer from the competition, and helps your audience evaluate their options to make the best decision. If your content does all these things, your chances of converting your audience skyrocket.

Strategic Distribution

Now that we've taken a look at what effective content looks like at each point during your audience's journey, let's discuss ways you can deliver that content directly to them at exactly the right moment.

To understand just how important strategic distribution is, imagine that you're on a hiking trail through the desert. You're thirsty but you're out of water, so your guide goes to get more. You continue walking. Time passes, and as you get farther along, you get more and more thirsty.

You call your guide, and he tells you that he's been waiting with the water at the place you started the trek. *What the hell?* You tell him that you're not anywhere near the starting point, that you kept walking to your destination. So he catches up with you, and you're relieved to finally have something to drink.

You put the bottle to your lips and taste coffee—not at all what you're looking for and not even close to what you need in this moment. You're frustrated, but he says he'll be right back with that water you asked for. So you give him one more chance.

More time passes, you keep hiking, and you still haven't gotten that water. It's literally all you need in this moment, and the person who is supposed to be helping you isn't where you need him. You call him, and he tells you that he's waiting for you at your destination already. Needless to say, this guy has no clue what he's doing, and you'll never hire him for a desert adventure again.

When it comes to populating the buyer's journey with high-impact content, you need to distribute the right content to the right place at the right time.

Being too salesy too early in the journey will scare off your prospect. Post a great article to a publication that your target buyer doesn't read and you'll achieve nothing. Although this sounds intuitive, the truth is, in many industries, 60 to 70 percent of content is not strategically distributed—most of it ends up sitting idly on company blogs that few people ever visit.[1]

Effective distribution connects your content with the right people at the right time and enables you to better hit the trust touch points that help you earn top-of-mind space. To make sure this happens, implement a distribution strategy that targets external publications, internal distribution, social media, and clients directly.

External Publications

My team and I have found that an effective way to get your audience to read your content is to publish it on the sites and blogs they're already reading. Does the audience you want to earn top-of-mind space with like reading *Inc.*? Maybe *Entrepreneur*? These sites have spent considerable time and resources building an engaged following. Create your content with those publication guidelines in mind, contribute it to the editor, and tap into its audience.

By doing this, you're simultaneously delivering content directly to this audience and being validated as a legitimate expert by virtue of your presence in that respected publication. This is especially important early on when you haven't yet built up the trust needed to draw your audience to your site.

When it comes to selecting target publications, bigger isn't necessarily better. Although getting a piece on the front page of the *Wall Street Journal* would certainly boost your reputation, it isn't exactly realistic. And even if you did land that front-page sweet spot, it probably wouldn't be as effective in the long run as publishing on a highly targeted, niche industry publication.

Sure, it doesn't sound as cool, but you'll earn more traction by speaking directly to the needs and interests of a smaller audience of highly engaged readers than a vast audience with scattered interests—and your content will be more effective.

Having published both on big-name platforms and on more niche sites, I have witnessed the power of a hypersegmented audience firsthand. For example, articles that my team and I post to smaller niche sites can outperform the content we publish in big marquee publications (in terms of lead generation, which is the primary goal we laid out in our strategy).

Don't let this deter you from pursuing marquee publications; the visibility can be very powerful, and you can still educate and engage members of those audiences. But you're better off building your strategy around consistent publishing through a diverse portfolio of external publications. As in an investment portfolio, you don't typically invest in only the Apples and Googles of the world; you want to diversify. Your publication strategy is similar. Diversify the sites between marquee, niche, trade, and so on, and see what works. Then go back to the sites that helped you reach the goals you set. This can not only help you meet your various goals, it can also help you meet your audiences at different parts of their journey.

Internal Distribution

Don't forget that your target reader isn't always exclusively your target buyer. If you're running a mature content initiative, you and your team will be pumping out a lot of content, and it's important that everyone on your team read it. It helps improve consistency in your messaging, keeps your team educated about your company or the industry, and optimizes the mileage of your content.

Let's say you run a software startup. Your head of operations publishes a piece about the lack of diversity in tech boardrooms and how nothing will change until the industry makes tangible commitments to addressing the issue. The piece goes live, but only a handful of people on your team read it. Later, your sales team is on a call with a prospect who mentions his company's commitment to hiring for diversity. Had your sales team read the piece, they could have forwarded it to the prospect, which might have gone a long way in forging a meaningful connection around a shared concern.

Missed opportunities like this one can add up. Fortunately, there are some powerful tools that make internal distribution seamless and streamlined. We have a Slack channel populated with our blog posts; whenever a new one is published, Zapier automation notifies the entire team and sends everyone a link to the article. Not only does this help keep everyone informed of what's happening internally, it sparks conversations about how various departments can best leverage and distribute our content to achieve their respective goals.

Social Media

A strong social distribution strategy can amplify the impact of your content exponentially. Social media provides multiple avenues for delivering your content directly to your audience, and it creates a space for rich, meaningful conversations that bolster your credibility and demonstrate your commitment to the audience.

Focus your social efforts on your target audience's preferred platforms. Does your target audience spend more time on Twitter than on LinkedIn? What about different audiences? For example, maybe Facebook is a better platform for posting and sharing content about your company culture for potential candidates, and maybe LinkedIn is better for generating leads.

An active, targeted presence on multiple platforms will increase the likelihood of your audience engaging with you, and taking the time to craft posts tailored to those specific platforms is a powerful invitation to interact with your content.

As you figure out what social sites to focus on, remember that LinkedIn—the platform as a whole, its groups, and its publishing platform—provides access to thriving communities that are segmented around industry and interest. Sharing with these networks is a great way to create conversations about your content and to connect with those who may well be a member of your specific target audience.

No matter what platform, you can assume that competition for attention is fierce. To ensure that your social efforts are on point, be diligent and thorough in testing your headlines and captions. Figure out what your audience finds compelling by analyzing click-through, sharing, and engagement rates. My team has found that combining quotes, stats, questions, and visuals yields the most effective results. Infographics are especially powerful; they garner three times as many likes and shares on average as any other type of content.[2] Don't forget to target editors and other curators of content in your industry in your social media efforts, and experiment with mentioning or tagging publications, editors, and influencers in your updates. This can increase your chances of syndication and improve redistribution opportunities.

Finally, consider budgeting for social promotion. At Influence & Co., we see the greatest conversion rates through LinkedIn and Twitter, so we buy LinkedIn Sponsored Updates and Promoted Tweets. The investment pays off for us. If you decide to go this route, make sure that you are constantly tracking success and evaluating the ROI.

Client Distribution

The fact that your current clients have already made it through the funnel doesn't mean that the funnel is complete. (Remember the inbound methodology from Chapter 1? The last step, Delight, refers to this idea that you can continue to add value, nurture, engage, and educate your audience even, and especially, after you've landed their business.)

Content can strengthen relationships with your existing customer base, which can boost brand loyalty and engagement. It can also open up discussions that lead clients to upgrade the services they're already buying from you—and also to refer other potential clients your way.

It's not difficult to deliver content to your current customers; you have an existing relationship, and, if you're doing your job right, they already trust you. That said, they'll only read your content if it's relevant and accessible.

We send our customers a weekly e-mail digest highlighting our best pieces, which helps keep them informed of industry trends as well as developments in our service offerings that can help them better achieve their goals. Maintaining an ongoing conversation with your clients through social media content is important, too; not only does it allow you to address their questions and concerns, it provides potential clients with insight into the level of customer care you provide. And the feedback you get from your customer base can help you shape your future content so that it is always useful, helpful, and relevant.

There are a lot of moving pieces to remember, which is why maintaining a checklist (a sample follows) can help you make sure that your content achieves maximum impact at every stage of the journey.

Tips for Maximizing Your Published Content

Content can add value to so many different areas of your company. Use this checklist to ensure you're getting the most out of your published content.

Marketing

☐ **Continuously share each piece of published content via social.** A few examples of ways to share your post include:
- The headline and the link
- A quote from the article
- A question
- Stats mentioned in the article

☐ **Comment on relevant conversations taking place in online forums and include a link to your post.** These forums can be found on LinkedIn Groups, Quora, or your favorite niche industry site.

☐ **Republish articles to your company blog or LinkedIn's publishing platform.** As long as you include a link back to the original to avoid duplicate content, repurposing can boost exposure and drive engagement.

☐ **Utilize paid search, social media, or a content distribution platform.** This will help you attract a larger but targeted audience for your content.

Sales

☐ **Prime and educate leads.** Your sales team can use content prior to sales conversations to educate leads, making the sales call more productive. Try sending over links to relevant published content to prime them for more effective and more meaningful calls.

☐ **Overcome objections.** Break down barriers by utilizing published content to help answer objections during sales conversations. When planning your content strategy, try to publish one piece of content that provides a solid answer to each objection your sales team encounters regularly.

☐ **Nurture leads.** We recommend utilizing an e-mail marketing campaign that references relevant published content to help nurture leads throughout the sales process.

Human Resources

☐ **Create a newsletter to share published content with your team.** You have a huge group of brand advocates within your company that can help promote and comment on your content.

☐ **Attract top talent and educate potential hires.** Teach future employees about your company culture and values by linking to a few relevant articles in a job posting.

☐ **Train new employees.** As you continue to grow your staff, published content lends itself more and more to the training process. Send new hires relevant content to give them insight into who your company leaders are and how your company positions itself.

Executive Branding

☐ **Link to published content in e-mail signatures.** Spruce up your e-mail signature to include a link to your favorite post or your most recent or most engaging article. It boosts organic visibility without being pushy.

☐ **Keep your personal social media accounts up to date.** Update your social media accounts, such as Twitter and LinkedIn, to include a list of the publications you're a contributor to. This will direct prospects to check out your work and naturally increase your credibility.

☐ **Share content with influencers.** Spark a conversation with people in your network by sharing your published content with them via e-mail. You'll increase views and network at the same time.

Personalizing Your Distribution

Personalization relates to strategic distribution, too. When you personalize content for your audience and place it on the publications and platforms that they're already reading and using, you strengthen that personalization. You make your audience feel like you're talking directly to them.

That's why picking the right platform for distribution is so important. The old days of traditional PR encouraged marketers to create a piece of content and farm it out to any outlet that would take it. If someone picked it up, you were good—but times have changed.

You don't need to create entirely different pieces of content for every person you're trying to reach, but you can personalize people's experiences in smaller ways. For example, I like to send individual e-mails to partners, clients, and other contacts I'm communicating with. Instead of plugging in my content and links to articles in an e-mail blast that only personalizes first names, I use a template that I create myself and quickly change a few key details for each message. So, when I wrote an article about barriers CMOs face with other executive team members, I attached it to an e-mail I'd templated for my CMO contacts and changed something as small as the intro. Instead of saying, "Hi, Rick!" my opening line said, "Hey, Rick. I hope things are going well for you and your family in Chicago."

Whether it's within the published content itself, where and how you distribute it, or simply in your correspondence, you've got plenty of chances to personalize your interactions. Take them.

The Importance of Actual Engagement, Not Just Distributing to Get Eyeballs

One of the most important things to remember when thinking about distribution is the difference between "views" and "engagement."

Someone who looks at a piece of content isn't necessarily engaging with it, which is manifested by reading it through to completion, staying on the page for a certain amount of time, commenting and sharing, or citing in future content pieces. The industry is realizing that a page view isn't really a way to build a relationship with an audience member. It's a surface-level metric that, on its own, isn't enough to get you top of mind.

Actual engagement is more desirable. Thankfully, technology has made it much easier to track these metrics more accurately than we've ever been able to. And because we have this ability, it'll be a growing focus for digital content and distribution in the future.

It definitely is for my team. Earlier, I mentioned the software that my team created, which we use for all our content—internally and for our clients—to track published performance. When we publish a piece of content, we're able to compare it to other content on the same publications and track performance by word count, style, day of the week, shares, and social reach as well as the finish rate on content published on our own site.

I'm very proud of what we've built; I think it's pretty impressive, and it's helped us in so many ways. But I can promise that these analytics are only going to advance over the next few years. I don't doubt that technology will be able to identify and measure every sort of behavior a reader displays when he or she interacts with any piece of digital content—which should result in better content and stronger relationships.

That's the real beauty: stronger relationships built on trust and consistent engagement with the audiences that matter most. Soon, content will be all about this level of trust and engagement, so understanding (and practicing) this mindset can prepare you for the future. Relationships will always have a strong impact on every aspect of your life—you have to understand and engage people, and do it consistently, to create opportunity.

Conclusion: Putting It into Practice

I think back to that conference I attended as a new CEO, when I couldn't connect with a single soul in the room. I remember what it was like to call my wife and break down in tears, afraid that launching Influence & Co. would prove to be the worst mistake of my life.

I wrote *Top of Mind* because I never want anyone to experience the desperation I felt in that moment. I honestly believe that having a top-of-mind mindset can help you create an environment where opportunities consistently come to you and trust barriers dissolve to make all areas of your life a little easier.

Part of what makes embracing a top-of-mind mindset so wonderful is how easy it can be. Helping others when you have the ability, being yourself, and doing it all with consistency are normal human behaviors. Don't get me wrong—it certainly takes time and commitment to put these behaviors into practice, to act on them enough that they become second nature, and to build and nurture personal relationships from them. But it is possible, and it can unlock countless opportunities—for business development, better relationships, personal growth, and more.

I used the example of written content as a vehicle for powering this mindset and applying it on a larger scale because I've experienced the benefits of this strategy firsthand. Through content, you can be helpful. You can share your knowledge, recognize others, and make people aware of opportunities. You can showcase your individual personality and your brand of likability. And with the right process, you can create content consistently enough to hit the right trust touch points, move yourself from short-term to long-term memory, and become top of mind with your audience.

On one level, this book is meant to be a practical guide for creating business opportunity. If you choose to read *Top of Mind* as a field manual, I am confident that implementing these strategies will help you grow your business. Even if you aren't diving headfirst into a full content strategy, by consistently communicating with your audience in an engaging way that they find valuable, you'll see a positive difference.

On another level, however, this book is about something much deeper and more personal. For me, achieving top-of-mind status is not the goal in and of itself. My goal is to create thriving, rich relationships. By focusing on making my relationships the best they can be, I'm able to prioritize what really matters to me—family, professional fulfillment, and friendship. My networks are packed full of people I genuinely care about, which makes nearly every interaction I have incredibly meaningful. There are many benefits to being emotionally invested in the lives of other people; top-of-mind status is simply one of them.

So I leave you with a challenge: As you apply the lessons of *Top of Mind* toward achieving your business goals, consider how you might use them to connect to people on a deeper level—team members, clients, friends, and family. What would happen if you put as much work into your relationships as you do into your work? How would your life change? What would the impact be on the people whom you love the most?

As we scramble to expand our networks, convert leads, and attract followers, it's easy to lose sight of our shared humanity. Focus on human connection and everything falls into place.

RESOURCE LIBRARY

Here is a list of tools and resources to help you become top of mind with your audience and achieve your goals. Please reach out to me and my team directly with any questions at topofmindhelp@gmail.com, and we'll do what we can to direct you to the right resources based on what success looks like to you.

Content Management, Relationship Management, Automation, and Workflow Tools

BuzzStream (http://www.buzzstream.com/)
    BuzzStream is an influencer outreach CRM and search engine that helps teams focused on SEO and PR build relationships with influencers, drive word-of-mouth traffic, and improve search performance.

ClearVoice (https://www.clearvoice.com/)
    ClearVoice is a content marketing platform and freelancer marketplace that uses technology to connect brands, creators, and publishers.

Constant Contact (https://www.constantcontact.com/)
    Constant Contact is an online marketing company that empowers small businesses and organizations to create and grow customer relationships and succeed through e-mail marketing.

Contactually (https://www.contactually.com/)

Contactually is a web-based CRM tool that turns relationships into results by helping maximize your network ROI, get more referrals, and gain more repeat business.

CoSchedule (http://coschedule.com)

CoSchedule is an ever-evolving content marketing Swiss Army knife that helps you plan and execute your content on a drag-and-drop editorial calendar, streamline internal communication, and save time.

DivvyHQ (https://divvyhq.com)

DivvyHQ is a cloud-based content planning, work flow, and collaboration tool built to help marketers and content producers get and stay organized and successfully execute demanding, complicated, and content-centric marketing initiatives.

Emma (http://myemma.com/)

Emma is an e-mail marketing tool that connects your data and builds your audience, and its Emma Plus e-mail automation platform helps marketing teams of all sizes do more with (and get more from) every aspect of their e-mail marketing.

HubSpot (https://www.hubspot.com/)

HubSpot is the leading inbound marketing and sales platform that helps companies attract visitors, convert leads, and close customers.

Infusionsoft (https://www.infusionsoft.com/)

Infusionsoft automates your small business's sales and marketing while combining your CRM, e-mail marketing, lead capture, and e-commerce in one place.

Kapost (https://kapost.com/)

Kapost is a B2B marketing platform that powers marketers to deliver compelling, consistent customer experiences by aligning content, people, and programs from first touch through sale to advocacy.

MailChimp (https://mailchimp.com/)

MailChimp is an e-mail marketing service that helps businesses of all sizes optimize their e-mail and e-commerce marketing with powerful and easy-to-use e-mail, marketing automation, and analytics tools that integrate with hundreds of popular applications and services.

Marketo (https://www.marketo.com/)

Marketo is the leader in digital marketing software solutions that helps marketers master the art and science of digital marketing and customer engagement.

Mixmax (https://mixmax.com/)

Mixmax is a productivity tool for Google that helps users send more engaging e-mails, customize templates, track e-mail opens, schedule messages, and ultimately build better relationships with the people in your network through improved communication.

ONTRAPORT (https://ontraport.com/)

ONTRAPORT provides a comprehensive business and marketing automation platform targeted to the specific needs of entrepreneurs and small businesses so users can easily start, systemize, and scale their businesses on a powerful platform integrating the marketing, sales, and business applications they need.

Pardot (http://www.pardot.com/)

Pardot is B2B marketing automation by Salesforce that allows marketing and sales teams to create, deploy, and manage online marketing campaigns through features, including CRM integration, lead management and nurturing, sales intelligence, and ROI reporting.

Salesforce (https://www.salesforce.com/)

Salesforce is the number one CRM platform that helps companies build more meaningful, lasting relationships with customers.

SalesforceIQ (formerly RelateIQ) (https://www.salesforceiq.com/)

SalesforceIQ is an out-of-the-box sales app and CRM for small businesses that uses data-driven insights to empower sales teams to sell smarter with Relationships Intelligence technology.

Zapier (https://zapier.com/)

Zapier makes it easy to automate tasks between apps online and connect apps and services to improve your productivity and business operations.

Content Creation and Distribution

Ceros (https://www.ceros.com/)

Ceros is a content marketing software platform encompassing a collaborative, real-time digital canvas upon which designers create animated, interactive content without the need for developers.

Contently (https://contently.com/)

Contently is a technology company that helps brands create great content at scale with smart technology, content strategy expertise, and a network of 50,000 freelance creatives.

Hootsuite (https://hootsuite.com/)

Hootsuite is a social relationship platform that empowers users to execute social media strategies across their organizations and social platforms and channels.

Influence & Co. (https://www.influenceandco.com/)

Influence & Co. is a content marketing agency that specializes in knowledge extraction and management to create and distribute engaging content that fuels companies' content marketing efforts and positions their key employees as influencers in their industries.

ion interactive (https://www.ioninteractive.com/)

ion interactive empowers modern marketers to produce engaging, interactive content marketing that generates higher-quality leads with an agile technology platform that launches, customizes, and tests all types of state-of-the-art interactive content marketing experiences without development resources.

NewsCred (http://www.newscred.com/)

NewsCred enables brands to easily manage content creation, distribution, and measurement—across channels, teams, and global markets—all on a single platform.

Quietly (https://www.quiet.ly/)

Quietly helps brands and publishers develop data-driven content that focuses on timeless topics to be promoted (and repromoted) to increase reach, traffic, and revenue by using proprietary tools and analytics, keyword trends, and competitive landscape research to shape evergreen content marketing opportunities.

Scripted (https://www.scripted.com)

Scripted offers freelance writing services from a network of thousands of industry-vetted writers to companies large and small to launch their content marketing efforts.

Skyword (http://www.skyword.com/)

Skyword moves brands—and their content—forward with a powerful combination of enterprise-class technology, authentic voices, and professional services and embraces a sustainable, scalable approach to original storytelling.

SnapApp (http://www.snapapp.com/)

SnapApp is an interactive content marketing platform that empowers marketers to create, deploy, manage, and measure a wide range of interactive content across multiple channels with full customization and design control to ensure content looks great on any device.

Sniply (https://snip.ly/)

Sniply is a social media conversion tool that adds custom calls to action to any page on the web, allowing users to engage followers and create conversion opportunities through every link they share.

Toptal (https://www.toptal.com/)

Toptal is an exclusive network of the top freelance software developers, designers, and finance experts in the world.

Search, Social, and Content Discovery

AddThis (http://www.addthis.com/)

AddThis is the leading provider of behavioral audience data and website marketing tools that help brands build more authentic customer relationships through insight, activation, and personalization products powered by the AddThis Audience Intelligence (Ai) platform.

Buffer (https://buffer.com/)

Buffer is a tool to schedule, optimize, and manage all your social media posts, photos, and videos to Instagram, Twitter, Facebook, Pinterest, LinkedIn, and Google+.

BuzzSumo (http://buzzsumo.com/)

BuzzSumo is a tool that provides social insights for content marketing and SEO campaigns by analyzing what topics, headlines, and content formats your audience shares, as well as analyzing your competitors' top content.

Dynamic Signal (https://dynamicsignal.com/)

Dynamic Signal is a social marketing company and leading employee communications platform that helps businesses consistently deliver relevant and personalized communications to their employees to ignite advocacy and engagement.

Kissmetrics (https://www.kissmetrics.com/)

Kissmetrics is an analytics and conversion solution built to help growth marketers measure revenue and customer behavior.

Likeable Local (http://www.likeablelocal.com/)

Likeable Local offers social media marketing software solutions that allow small businesses to create, enhance, and manage their social media presence.

MavSocial (http://mavsocial.com/)

MavSocial is a social publishing and analytics tool designed to help brands and agencies create, manage, and promote visual and media content on social channels.

Moz (https://moz.com/)

Moz develops inbound marketing software, provides robust APIs for link data and social influence, and hosts the web's most vibrant community of online marketers.

Outbrain (http://www.outbrain.com/)

Outbrain is the world's largest content discovery platform, bringing personalized, relevant mobile and video content to audiences while helping publishers understand their audiences through data.

PostBeyond (https://postbeyond.com/)

PostBeyond bridges the gaps in workforce communications systems to deliver a modern work experience and engage your employee advocates by enabling employees and partners to post approved brand content to their personal networks in an efficient, consistent, and measurable way.

Revcontent (https://www.revcontent.com/)

Revcontent is the world's fastest-growing content recommendation and native advertising network, powering 250 billion content recommendations a month.

Searchmetrics (http://www.searchmetrics.com/)

Searchmetrics is a search and content optimization platform that provides customers with competitive advantage, helps identify new business opportunities by highlighting content consumers are engaging with on industry and competitor sites, and offers suggestions for content creation that improves relevance and boosts conversions.

SEMrush (www.semrush.com)

SEMrush is a leading competitive keyword and AdWords research tool that helps users learn about their (and their competitors') digital marketing campaigns.

Smarp (http://www.smarp.com/)

Smarp is an employee communication, advocacy, and engagement app that brings company news and content to the fingertips of employees, keeping teams up to date, engaging them to communicate, and helping them share their knowledge with their own social networks.

Socedo (http://www.socedo.com/)

Socedo is a demand generation system that empowers B2B marketers to discover, engage, and qualify prospects through social media to increase revenue at scale.

SocialOomph (https://www.socialoomph.com/)

SocialOomph provides a free and paid productivity service for social media that allows users to organize and analyze Twitter accounts in one place while also tracking keywords, mentions, and retweets across multiple accounts.

SocialRank (https://socialrank.com/)

SocialRank makes it easy to understand, organize, identify, segment, and manage users' most engaged, valuable followers on Instagram and Twitter.

Sprout Social (http://sproutsocial.com/)

Sprout Social is a social media management, analytics, engagement, and CRM tool that helps businesses grow their social presence and audience.

Taboola (https://www.taboola.com/)

Taboola is the leading content discovery platform that provides publishers the option to display content recommendations in three ways: with content discovery widgets, in-stream native ads, or a hybrid, displaying articles, videos, slideshows, and other content, both from within the site and from other advertisers and publishers.

TweetDeck (https://tweetdeck.twitter.com/)

TweetDeck is a social media dashboard app for Twitter that offers improved user experience and greater flexibility by allowing users to view multiple timelines in one interface, manage multiple accounts, schedule and manage posts, and more.

WordStream (https://www.wordstream.com/)

WordStream provides software and services to help online marketers maximize the performance of their paid search and social campaigns, driving traffic, leads, and sales for lower costs by automating proven best practices and delivering expert-level results in a fraction of the time for campaigns on Google AdWords, Bing, and Facebook.

PR Resources

AirPR (https://www.airpr.com/)

AirPR is the leading industry educator and technology solution that helps businesses better measure PR's impact by providing analytics, insights, and measurement solutions for the evolving PR industry.

Cision (http://www.cision.com/us/)

Cision is a leading media communication technology and analytics company that enables marketers and communicators to effectively manage their earned media programs in coordination with paid and owned channels to drive business impact.

PRWeb (http://service.prweb.com/home/)

PRWeb is an online press release distribution network that helps you create buzz, increase online visibility, and drive website traffic.

These are some of the most common and trusted resources used by me, my team, and others I trust. Again, please reach out to me at topofmindhelp@gmail.com if you need any assistance connecting to the right solution for your business.

NOTES

Chapter 1

1   BI Intelligence, "Ad-Block Software Is Approaching 200 Million Users—Here's How Publishers Are Reacting," *Business Insider*, September 29, 2015, http://www.businessinsider.com/ad-blocking-software-has-200-million-users-2015-8?op=1.

2   PageFair Team, "The 2015 Ad Blocking Report," *PageFair* (blog), August 10, 2015, https://pagefair.com/blog/2015/ad-blocking-report/.

3   Bryan Kramer, "There Is No More B2B or B2C: It's Human to Human," *Bryan Kramer* (blog), January 27, 2014, http://www.bryankramer.com/there-is-no-more-b2b-or-b2c-its-human-to-human-h2h/.

4   Lisa Gevelber, "Why Consumer Intent Is More Powerful Than Demographics," December 2015, https://www.thinkwithgoogle.com/articles/why-consumer-intent-more-powerful-than-demographics.html.

5   HubSpot, "The Inbound Methodology," https://research.hubspot.com/reports/the-state-of-inbound-2015.

6   HubSpot, "State of Inbound 2015," http://www.stateofinbound.com.

7   Lori Wizdo, "Buyer Behavior Helps B2B Marketers Guide the Buyer's Journey," *Lori Wizdo's Blog*, Forrester, October 4, 2012, http://blogs.forrester.com/lori_wizdo/12-10-04-buyer_behavior_helps_b2b_marketers_guide_the_buyers_journey.

8   Laurie Beasley, "Why It Takes 7 to 13+ Touches to Deliver a Qualified Sales Lead (Part 1)," OMI, October 10, 2013, https://www.onlinemarketinginstitute.org/blog/2013/10/why-it-takes-7-to-13-touches-to-deliver-a-qualified-sales-lead-part1/.

9   CareerBuilder, *How to Rethink the Candidate Experience and Make Better Hires*, http://resources.careerbuilder.com/guides/candidate-experience-guide.

Chapter 2

1   Jeff Jones, "The Truth Hurts," *LinkedIn*, May 13, 2014, https://www.linkedin.com/pulse/20140513221110-3501295-the-truth-hurts.

2   Jeff Haden, "How to Be Exceptionally Likable: 11 Things the Most Charming People Always Do," *Inc.*, December 22, 2015, http://www.inc.com/jeff-haden/how-to-be-exceptionally-likable-11-things-the-most-charming-people-always-do.html.

3   Tim Urban, "Elon Musk: The World's Raddest Man," *Wait but Why* (blog), May 7, 2015, http://waitbutwhy.com/2015/05/elon-musk-the-worlds-raddest-man.html.

4 John Hall, "4 C-Suite Objections to Content Marketing and How to Overcome Them," *Forbes*, December 1, 2013, http://www.forbes.com/sites/johnhall/2013 /12/01/4-c-suite-objections-to-content-marketing-and-how-to-overcome -them/#15ad4bd97a02.

Chapter 3

1 Shane Snow, "The Rise of the Superconnector," April 2, 2013, http://www.fast company.com/3007657/rise-superconnector.
2 Just e-mail topofmindhelp@gmail.com, and someone from Influence & Co. will respond with an answer for you—and, many times, even an introduction or discount code to help you get started.
3 MediaKix Team, "How Brands Can Reach New Audiences with Micro-Influencers," June 29, 2016, http://mediakix.com/2016/06/micro-influencers-definition -marketing/#gs.wFYUzm8.
4 These are just a few of the tools that can help you manage your relationships. Check out the Resource Library at the end of this book or shoot me an e-mail at topof mindhelp@gmail.com for recommendations.
5 Again, if you're looking for recommendations for this practice, reach out to topof mindhelp@gmail.com, and I can connect you to the right resources.
6 You can check out topof mindbook.com/resources for customizable spreadsheet templates my team created to make this process simpler for you and to reference our software recommendations.

Chapter 4

1 Brené Brown, "The Power of Vulnerability," filmed June 2010, TED video, https:// www.ted.com/talks/brene_brown_on_vulnerability?language=en#t-406950.
2 MarketingCharts, "Honesty Is the Best Corporate Policy," January 27, 2010, http:// www.marketingcharts.com/traditional/honesty-is-the-best-corporate-policy -11762/.
3 Jodi Kantor and Avid Streitfeld, "Inside Amazon: Wrestling Big Ideas in a Bruising Workplace," *New York Times*, August 15, 2015, http://www.nytimes .com/2015/08/16/technology/inside-amazon-wrestling-big-ideas-in-a-bruising -workplace.html.
4 Nick Ciubotariu, "An Amazonian's Response to 'Inside Amazon: Wrestling Big Ideas in a Bruising Workplace,'" LinkedIn, August 16, 2015, https://www.linkedin .com/pulse/amazonians-response-inside-amazon-wrestling-big-ideas-nick -ciubotariu.
5 December 17, 2015, http://qz.com/571151/the-mast-brothers-fooled-the-world -into-buying-crappy-hipster-chocolate-for-10-a-bar/.
6 Tim Cook, "A Message to Our Customers," Apple, February 16, 2016, http://www .apple.com/customer-letter/.
7 You can download a knowledge bank template to start storing and organizing your team's knowledge here: offers.influenceandco.com/knowledge-management -landing-page. You can also browse the Resource Library in this book for other software options.

8 Nadav Klein and Ed O'Brien, "The Tipping Point of Moral Change: When Do Good and Bad Acts Make Good and Bad Actors?" *Social Cognition* 34, no. 2 (July 2016):149–66, http://home.uchicago.edu/~nklein/MoralTippingPoint.pdf.

Chapter 5

1 Ajay Banga, "Financial Inclusion by 2020: Our Generation's Equivalent of Putting a Man on the Moon," LinkedIn, November 12, 2013, https://www.linkedin.com/pulse/20131112154659-283931055-financial-inclusion-by-2020-our-generation-s-equivalent-of-putting-a-man-on-the-moon.

2 Southtree, "10 Unforgettable Statistics About Human Memory," April 21, 2015, https://southtree.com/memories-matter/statistics-about-human-memory.

3 Alison Preston, "How Does Short-Term Memory Work in Relation to Long-Term Memory?" *Scientific American*, September 26, 2007, http://www.scientificamerican.com/article/experts-short-term-memory-to-long-term/.

4 Amos Tversky and Daniel Kahneman, "Availability: A Heuristic for Judging Frequency and Probability," *Cognitive Psychology* 5, no. 2 (September 1973): 207–32, http://www.sciencedirect.com/science/article/pii/0010028573900339.

5 Kelsey Meyer, "Does Thought Leadership Ever End?" Influence & Co., October 6, 2015, https://blog.influenceandco.com/does-thought-leadership-ever-end.

Chapter 6

1 Content Marketing Institute, "B2B Content Marketing 2016 Benchmarks, Budgets, and Trends—North America," 2015, http://contentmarketinginstitute.com/wp-content/uploads/2015/09/2016_B2B_Report_Final.pdf.

2 Jonathan Becher, "The Psychology of the To-Do List," *Forbes*, March 17, 2014, http://www.forbes.com/sites/sap/2014/03/17/the-psychology-of-the-to-do-list/#42ae71ab3a37.

3 If you don't want to build a team around you, then hire the resources you need to get the job done. (I actually hire my own company to do this for me because of my time constraints and challenges with writing.) No matter what, work out a collaborative creative process that uses everyone's strengths to execute.

4 Ulrich Boser, "The Power of the Pygmalion Effect: Teachers Expectations Strongly Predict College Completion," Center for American Progress, October 6, 2014, https://www.americanprogress.org/issues/education/report/2014/10/06/96806/the-power-of-the-pygmalion-effect/.

5 Christopher Heine, "How IBM Got 1,000 Staffers to Become Brand Advocates on Social Media," *Adweek*, July 1, 2015, http://www.adweek.com/news/technology/how-ibm-got-1000-staffers-become-brand-advocates-social-media-165664.

6 The tools listed in the Resource Library of this book, as well as those available at topofmindbook.com/resources can offer assistance to maximize your content distribution.

Chapter 7

1 And it's worked for us. As a result, you can now search terms such as "content marketing companies" and "thought leadership companies" and find that our company consistently shows up. We've grown closer and closer to creating that content utopia.

Chapter 8

1 Simon Sinek, "How Great Leaders Inspire Action," filmed September 2009, TED video, https://www.ted.com/talks/simon_sinek_how_great_leaders_inspire _action?language=en.

2 I personally love this exercise, and I encourage you to give it a try, too. Does your company's communication truly communicate that *why*? Is that at the core of your content strategy? Do you personally communicate that *why* when you're interacting with customers and partners?

When I last went through this exercise, I realized that I often got stuck on the *how* or the *what* and didn't always get to the why, which is the most vital element of any communication strategy.

3 The Economist Group, "Missing the Mark: Global Content Survey of Brand Marketers and Their B2B Audiences," 2014, http://www.missingthemark.ads.economist .com/presentation.

4 Sumi Krishnan, "5 Powerful Rules for Women Entrepreneurs to Live By," *Entrepreneur*, April 6, 2015, https://www.entrepreneur.com/article/244402.

5 Dustin McKissen, "Five Reasons Why I'm Not Sleeping in My Car Anymore," LinkedIn, October 22, 2014, https://www.linkedin.com/pulse/20141022144703 -197220852-five-reasons-why-i-m-not-sleeping-in-my-car-anymore.

Chapter 9

1 Daniel Roth, "Why Vocal Employees Are a Company's Best PR," FastCompany .com, March 25, 2015, http://www.fastcompany.com/3044156/hit-the-ground -running/why-vocal-employees-are-a-companys-best-pr.

2 Maya Luke, "4 Ways to Jumpstart Your Content Strategy Next Quarter," Influence & Co. (blog), February 16, 2016, https://blog.influenceandco.com/4-ways-to-jump start-your-content-strategy-next-quarter.

3 The software options listed in the Resource Library should shed light on tools that can help you execute and scale your referral program, but for any recommendations (or more insight into how we do it), you can e-mail topofmindhelp @gmail.com.

Chapter 10

1 Patrick Welch, "Moneyball: Use Content Intelligence and Analytics to Build a Successful Sales Team," Content Marketing Institute, February 6, 2015, http:// contentmarketinginstitute.com/2015/02/moneyball-content-sales-team/.

2 Jesse Mawhinny, "37 Visual Content Marketing Statistics You Should Know in 2016," *Where Marketers Go to Grow* (blog), January 13, 2016, https://blog.hubspot .com/marketing/visual-content-marketing-strategy.

INDEX

ABOUT THE AUTHOR

JOHN HALL is the cofounder and CEO of Influence & Co., a firm that helps brands and individuals extract and leverage their expertise to create, publish, and distribute content to gain influence, visibility, and credibility with their key audiences. Influence & Co. has become one of the largest providers of expert content to online publications.

In 2016, John was one of the recipients of the EY Entrepreneur of the Year Award for "Best Emerging Company" and was recognized as one of the *Business Journal*'s Top 100 Visionaries, while Influence & Co. was ranked No. 239 on the Inc. 500 and No. 72 on the *Forbes* list of the "Most Promising Companies in America." It was also recognized at the United Nations for being Empact's "Best Marketing and Advertising Company of 2014."

John has been called "one of the most powerful people in media who you've never met" by Inc.com and a "must-see keynote speaker" by Forbes.com. He is mentioned consistently in major publications as a top influencer, leader, and speaker. John writes weekly columns for Forbes.com and Inc.com and has contributed to more than 50 online publications, including Harvard Business Review, Entrepreneur, Fast Company, and Mashable.

As much as he'd love to cover his mom's refrigerator with these accomplishments, what's most important to him is helping others and paying it forward. Feel free to reach out to him if you think he can be helpful.

When John isn't working, he loves spending time with his beautiful wife, Lindsay, and their two adorable daughters.

For more information, visit influenceandco.com.